THAT DOES IT

Desperate Reflections on American Culture

Peter Heinegg

Hamilton Books
A member of
The Rowman & Littlefield Publishing Group
Lanham · Boulder · New York · Toronto · Plymouth, UK

Copyright © 2009 by
Hamilton Books
4501 Forbes Boulevard
Suite 200
Lanham, Maryland 20706
Hamilton Books Acquisitions Department (301) 459-3366

Estover Road
Plymouth PL6 7PY
United Kingdom

All rights reserved
Printed in the United States of America
British Library Cataloging in Publication Information Available

Library of Congress Control Number: 2008936234
ISBN-13: 978-0-7618-4393-1 (paperback : alk. paper)
ISBN-10: 0-7618-4393-0 (paperback : alk. paper)
eISBN-13: 978-0-7618-4394-8
eISBN-10: 0-7618-4394-9

∞™ The paper used in this publication meets the minimum
requirements of American National Standard for Information
Sciences—Permanence of Paper for Printed Library Materials,
ANSI Z39.48—1984

To the memory of my parents:

*my father, born Friedrich (Fritz) Feilchenfeld,
in Vienna, Mar. 3, 1914,*

died in Delhi, NY, December 4, 2002

and

*my mother, born Arlene Ellsworth Willis
in The Bronx, Oct. 29, 1921,*

died in Cooperstown, NY Feb. 1, 1997

They got my hopes up, but they taught me to be critical

America is the most grandiose experiment the world has seen . . . but, I am afraid, it is not going to be a success.

—Sigmund Freud in Ronald W. Clark,
Freud, The Man and The Cause (1980)

Contents

Acknowledgments		vii
Introduction: America, Love It or Lambaste It (or Both)		ix
1.	Paddling Through the Deluge	1
2.	Loonyland	7
3.	Scoundrels Swarming in the Last Refuge	11
4.	A Nation of Make-Believers	17
5.	Natural Splendor, National Squalor	23
6.	Throwing Our Weight Around	27
7.	Wait, There's More!	31
8.	The Amerigun Way of Life	35
9.	From Barbarism to Decadence Without Passing through You-Know-What	41
10.	Hats Off, Guys	45
11.	The Canting of America	49
12.	It's Offal, It's Awful, It's All We've Got	53
13.	Sludge, Slime, and Saccharine	57
14.	What We're Really Good At	63
15.	"News" You Can "Use"	67
16.	Feelthy Peektures of All-American Guys and Gals	71
17.	Mothers, Don't Let Your Daughters Grow Up to be Blondes	75
18.	Up Close and Personal—Yecch	79
19.	Conservatism, Face to Face	83
20.	Culture is So Over	89
21.	Wigger Nation	93
22.	American Catholics and Other Bright Lights	99
23.	Sexual Wisdom from the Horse's Ass	105
24.	Had Enough?	111
About the Author		119

Acknowledgments

I wish to thank Shelby Singelton Music, Inc. and Quicket Publishing Co., Nashville, Tennessee for permission to quote "The Battle Hymn of Lt. Calley" by James M. Smith and Julian Wilson, as well as OnTheIssues.org Copyright 2008 The Speakout Foundation for material on the voting record of Rep. Lamar Smith.

Introduction

America, Love It or Lambaste It (or Both)

> How fading and insipid do all objects accost us, that are not conveyed in the vehicle of delusion! how shrunk is everything, as it appears in the glass of nature! So that if it were not for the assistance of artificial mediums, false lights, refracted angles, varnish, and tinsel, there would be a mighty level in the felicity and enjoyments of mortal men. If this were seriously considered by the world, as I have a certain reason to suspect it hardly will, men would no longer reckon among their high points of wisdom, the art of exposing weak sides, and publishing infirmities.
>
> —Jonathan Swift, *A Tale of a Tub* (1704)

> And when we come together and work together, there is no limit to the greatness of America. (Applause.)
>
> —George W. Bush, Acceptance speech (Nov. 3, 2004)

For the past thirty-five years or so I've spent at least one term teaching *Gulliver's Travels* and other works by Jonathan Swift. Over that time, Dean Swift, the unbelieving Christian priest, the brilliant abuser of his own species, the poet-prophet-lunatic, has become my father in the (un)faith. Swift's *saeva indignatio* is, I believe, the only rational response to the crazy world he was born into—and the much crazier world that I/we have inherited. I make no claim to any of Swift's sublime gifts, just to his rage at the mess humans have made of the planet, and to his seeking relief in continual mockery. If you can't beat 'em, jab 'em.

This book is a collection of essays, a volley of Parthian shots (as I hightail it off into old age and death), aimed at the bad behavior, stupid, vicious or both, of my congeners in the most deluded First World country on the planet, USA, *Prases populusque Americanus*. It's also a series of variations on themes I first developed in *Better Than Both: The Case for Pessimism* (2004). As I mentioned there, America has a very limited tolerance for negative thinking. Imagine a presidential candidate striding up to a bank of microphones and announcing, "Well, I'm a pessimist, and so . . ." End of story, tarred and feathered. One of these days we're going to become an old country; but in the meantime we still stress—and like to think we have a quasi-monopoly on—all the virtues of youth: openness, vitality, resilience, and a dazzling menu of options and possibilities. As a result we have no patience with nay-sayers. If there's something wrong (and what the hell, we know we're not perfect), then stop complaining and fix it. But what if there's no fix in sight—or in existence? Well, in that case, say I, you can always curse.

But, wait a minute, history (and especially *our* history) is full of success stories, of problems faced and overcome. "We" ended slavery (accidentally, in 1863), gave women the vote (belatedly, in 1920), returned the Canal Zone to Panama (reluctantly, in 1979), cured polio and stuff. Who knows, we may eventually get around to repealing the death penalty, idiotic drug laws, our plutocratic tax code, legalized homophobia, and the proliferation of handguns. So, roll up your sleeves America, and get to work.

Then again, the saner response might be to do your best, but—in view of our present record, our current miseries, and our dismal future prospects—start cracking wise, and let it all hang out. I mean, for instance, it's 2008 and Mormonism is the fastest-growing religion in America, which since the death of Lincoln has been governed mostly by knaves and fools. As inequities between the rich and the poor grow worse, people are having fierce debates about banning same-sex marriage. As millions die from AIDS, the US government sermonizes about abstinence, demented Islamic fundamentalism flourishes, and tens of millions of African women undergo clitoridectomies. As the planet fatally heats up, as it gets plundered and polluted, and a massive population crash becomes more and more likely, Americans piggishly squander resources as never before. Traditional religions mouth their fantasies about an obviously dead God (who is nonetheless 100% on our side); and most of what popular culture serves up is dreck. Our national discourse is awash in fuzzy mantras and clichés—"God bless America," "family values" "relationships," even "freedom" and "democracy," and, if all else fails, the American Dream—as opposed to serious analysis. (See Chapter 11, "The Canting of America.")

Perhaps the most galling feature of all this is that so few people acknowledge it. Here we are in 2008, and a large minority of Americans still think we were attacked on 9/11 by Saddam Hussein and his henchmen. A majority would like to see the Ten Commandments posted in our public schools and creationism taught alongside evolution. Americans believe we give vast chunks of our GNP in foreign aid (the actual figure is .17%) to the world's poor. Americans gladly and repeatedly vote—*if* they vote at all—for a string of unbelievable dolts from Bush and Cheney to lesser known disasters like Senator Jim DeMint and Rep. Lamar Smith (see Chapter 19, "Conservatism, Face to Face"). Americans are cheerful ignoramuses (listen to the natives interviewed on Jay Leno's "Jaywalking" rambles through Darkest L.A.), who are paradoxically convinced of their matchless collective wisdom. Americans consume, literally and figuratively, prodigious quantities of junk (sometimes combining both kinds of poisonous intake, for example. by stuffing themselves with salted, buttered popcorn while watching some God-awful flick (*Snakes on a Plane? Basic Instinct 2? Chuck and Larry?*) at home or the local multiplex. (See Chapter 12, "It's Offal, It's Awful, It's All We've Got.")

But, above all, Americans are *unaware*—or, as everybody says nowadays, clueless. A supremely pragmatic people, they love know-*how*; but they're not much given to asking why. And, as de Tocqueville noted almost two centuries ago, they're hypersensitive to criticism: you can mock politicians forever, but you can't mock the fools who elect them. A little muckraking is fine, but by and large satire remains what closes Saturday night. Year after year my students scratch their head at the ferocity of Swift's "Digression on Madness" from *A Tale of a Tub*: "Wow, this guy is SO negative." You bet, kids: negative and desperately right. (Now imagine him brought back to life, strapped into a chair, and forced to watch Fox News or *Cops* or *America's Funniest Home Videos*. American culture, it seems to me, is both loony and complacent, hence pretty much impervious to criticism. What follows, accordingly, will be a stream of reasoned, fair-minded abuse, or what Tacitus would have called *ira et studium* (there being next to no room, alas, for Swift's beloved "sweetness and light").

One final introductory note: whatever their flaws/crime/horrors, it might be (sensibly) argued, America and its culture are still part of the planetary continuum, and have no copyright on any of those vices. Then too, the overwhelming majority of us came from somewhere else, so why not trace all the trouble back to its European and Asian roots? In any case, as most of the Third World descends more or less precipitously into hell, only a lunatic would deny that it's better to live here than, say, Sierra Leon, Somalia, Kyrgyzstan, Bangladesh, or, for that matter, Belarus.

Suicide bombings, murder and kidnapping are far less prevalent in Dallas than in Baghdad Rates of honor killing and stoning for adultery are low. The pursuit of happiness continues hereabouts, not quite undisturbed, but in a semi-doable mode for many folks in the better-off classes. Enough whining already!

Sure, sure, sure. BUT: 1) This is the culture that 300 million of us are de facto trapped in and suffering from; 2) It carries tremendous weight and influence elsewhere, as anyone who's ever flown beyond these shores will have noticed; 3) It's among the most triumphantly self-congratulatory of cultures, and hence among the most deserving to be pelted with rotten eggs. Duck!

Chapter 1

Paddling Through the Deluge

> The *positive* evils and dangers of the representative, as of every other form of government, may be reduced to two heads: first, general ignorance and incapacity, or, to speak more moderately, insufficient mental qualifications, in the controlling body; secondly, the danger of its being under the influence of interests not identical with the general welfare of the community.
> —J.S. Mill, *Representative Government*, VI

Note: the following screed was written in December 2005, in the wake of George W. Bush's catastrophic re-election. By the time it appears in print, close to the end of the Bush years, the harm done by the Bushies will have reached new levels of toxicity. Thanks to his non-stop schuss down the slopes of popular favor, attacking the Decider will be easier than ever; but the vast bulk of the attackers will likely treat him as a goofy accident. Few conservative commentators will voice any deep buyer's remorse, and few liberals will admit to rage at the countless millions—half of the country, let's say—who put and kept Bush in office. It's all *his* fault—but of course it isn't and it wasn't.

By the spring of 2006 Dubya was already being called the worst president in American history, an honor hitherto accorded to the likes of Warren Harding, James Buchanan or U.S. Grant (see below). In any case, Bush will surely have been the most mocked, caricatured, and contemptuously put-down political figure in living memory, with whole regions of late-night comedy shows, cable TV, and the blogosphere devoted to trashing him. Yet, for all the fury (and accuracy) of this critical fusillade, what good will it have done as of January, 2009, when Bush &

Co.'s horrific show finally closes? Railing, one can only hope, may prove therapeutic.

Wintry Thoughts, January, 2005

Grant fretted and irritated him, like the *Terebratula*, as a defiance of first principles. He had no right to exist. He should have been extinct for ages. The idea that, as society grew older, it grew one-sided, upset evolution and made of education a fraud. That, two thousand years after Alexander the Great and Julius Caesar, a man like Grant should be called—and should actually and truly be—the highest product of the most advanced evolution, made evolution ludicrous. One must be as commonplace as Grant's own commonplaces to maintain such an absurdity. The progress of evolution from President Washington to President Grant, was alone evidence enough to upset Darwin.

—*The Education of Henry Adams*, Ch. XVII

Thus Henry Adams' famous recoil of disgust in early 1869 when he heard the list of appointees to Ulysses S. Grant's first cabinet. The Grant administration proved, of course, to be just as venal and inept as its worst enemies predicted. But Grant had been a great general, and in his last years he became a great writer, as evidenced by his *Personal Memoirs*. For the rest of the 19th century, in fact, the White House was inhabited by a collection of losers who have slipped into richly deserved oblivion.

135 years later, after the re-election of George W. Bush, a draft-dodging chicken hawk rather than a brave warrior, but with more power at his command than Grant could have dreamed of, a reformed alcoholic spouting lies and clichés rather than a unreformed alcoholic with real dignity and natural eloquence, many Americans are feeling the Henry Adams blues. Is *this* what the country has come to?

Yup, it has; and the only response I can personally muster is a mixture of initial rage and ultimate contempt. The rage diminishes as I recall the election and re-election of Richard Nixon (now often spoken of as great-but-flawed) and Ronald Reagan (now throning to non-stop hurrahs in the national pantheon), the one-term reign of Poppy Bush and the fiasco of 2000. Men and women my age (66) have seen a whole generation's quartet of dreadful leaders (with a sickening retinue of toadies and hitmen) endorsed by Their Majesties, the American people; so that what we're looking at is the rule, not the exception. The bulk of our adult lives has been spent with fools, knaves, and worse ensconced in the Oval office, God damn them all.

True, only about half of those eligible to vote actually showed up at the polls from the late '60s onward, and the 2000 election was stolen; but the fact that so many millions of by and large sane persons could vote for candidates who were both objectively awful and intrinsically hostile to many of their supporters' own interests serves as another demonstration of the vices of American democracy. In Book VI of *The Republic* Plato compares the democratic ruler to an animal trainer, who studies the "huge and powerful beast" with great care, learns all its idiosyncracies, and calls this experience wisdom.

Which sounds like Karl Rove *avant la lettre*. There are a number of ways to respond to this situation. One is the usual TV news show pundit's (Cokie Roberts', say) admiration for the Bushies' brilliant gamesmanship. Politics *is* a sport, isn' t it? And winning isn't everything, it's the only thing, yadda yadda yadda. Democrats are chided, by turns, for losing touch with the soccer moms (bless them) or white males (Joe Six-Pack & Co.) or Hispanics or Evangelicals or Roman Catholics or the values-gang or otherwise tolerant heterosexuals troubled by the prospect of gay marriage (though they regularly catch, or used to catch, *Will and Grace* or *Queer Eye for the Straight Guy*). Whatever, the Dems' animal-training skills are constantly being shown up as rusty-to-non-existent.

Of course, for true partisans none of this will do. The notion that a smarter campaign (run a more aggressive national convention far from Boston, instantly blast the Swift Boat Veterans disinformation, harp on Dubya's flip-flopping) can't get around the disgusting fact that even if Kerry had won by a whisker or two, tens of millions of Americans would still have voted for Bush. And even if one deducts from the majority all the people whose self-interest automatically dyed them red (nouveau riche millionaires, defense contractors, religious fanatics, Texans, etc.), there remains a vast horde of cretins dumb enough to feel safe in the hands of Bush's foreign policy, to bury their doubts about 9/11/, the war (did you say 100,000-600,000 Iraqis dead?—whatever), the deficit, health care, the environment, and so on, to hand the nation over to a vicious oligarchy for four more years of gang rape. Likewise, a Kerry victory wouldn't by itself have removed the intransigent, self-righteous, rabid Republican majorities in the House and Senate or change the damned-if-you-do/damned-if-you-don't situation in Iraq. The envelope announcing Democratic success in 2004 might have contained a letter-bomb. In any case what's done is done (P.S.—and the Democratic victories in 2006 haven't done much to change it).

Given those facts, the options are few and unappetizing. One might go into internal exile (wake me up for the Beijing Olympics, at the earliest). One could—actually must—grab for the remote whenever Mitch McConnell, Tony Snow, Condoleezza Rice, or anyone to the right of Tim Russert appears on TV. One—at any rate, some rich or venturesome individuals—might simply leave the country to seek asylum in, say, Toronto or London or Stockholm. and watch America's patriotic dementia and plutocratic orgies from a safe distance. One might spend more time listening to brain-dead right-wing oracles making fools of themselves. (Not so long ago on CNN Judith Riesman accused Alfred Kinsey of bringing about "the moral demise of America," a process apparently to be sealed forever by his celluloid stand-in, Liam Neeson.) Or, and this is my favorite, one might settle for *Schadenfreude*, waiting and watching for Bush's (Rumsfeld's, Cheney's, Ashcroft's, DeLay's) ideological chickens come home to roost, as they surely will. The US *will* lose the war in Iraq; our arrogance *will* foment more terrorism; Christian crazies *will* flood the courts and schools; civil rights (and abortion rights?) *will* be savaged; workers *will* get shafted; the Wal-Martization of America *will* proceed by leaps and bounds. And we told you so. Take THAT, subscribers to the *Wall Street Journal* and fans of Fox News!

Needless to say, enjoying the prospects of such a devolution is morally (and otherwise) dubious. Millions of innocent people will be made to suffer, at home and abroad. But that's as inevitable as it is deplorable; and at least some of the victims will have called their misery down on themselves through electoral karma. Ditto for all Republicans with incomes too low to cash in on the Bush tax cuts or to afford health insurance. As the Spanish proverb has it, when the poor give to the rich, the devil laughs. Well, Satan must be fairly doubled over in hysterics these days; and Democrats lucky enough to be shielded from the worst of the Bush injustices can share a little bit of his glee. It was, appropriately enough, the arch-conservative Joseph de Maistre who said that each nation has the government it deserves. And, in the end even the rich and powerful Bushies may end up suffering, psychically anyhow, from the massive failure and disgrace that will be their mean-spirited legacy. Let's hope so.

But, beyond the cold-hearted pleasures of "You asked for it," there's another cause for rueful satisfaction in the Bush triumph. Perhaps because of their long involvement with Christian theology, Americans seem to learn nothing except through a process of sin-and-belated-repentance. There was no OSHA till industrial accidents had killed and maimed thousands of workers. The country had to poison itself with DDT before a prophet like Rachel Carson could arise to call for a turnabout. Same thing with unsafe Corvairs and (yecch) Ralph Nader. So, let the land stagger down the primrose path to disaster, if that's what it takes for the national co nscience to kick in.

On the other hand, what if the operative model here is Greek-tragic, not Hebrew-scriptural? What if we're heading, not to a return from a cruel and bloody exile, but to a disastrous comeuppance or, more likely, a series of them? Well, if this *were* a Greek tragedy, only the upper-class protagonists would suffer, while the chorus looked on and shook its collective head. But that, obviously, is not how things work, Brace yourselves, folks—or start packing.

Chapter 2

Loonyland

- % of American adults held in either prisons or mental institutions in 1953 and today, respectively: 0.67, 0.68
- % of these adults in 1953 who were in mental institutions: 75
- % today who are in prisons: 97
- Estimated amount that poor US adults cost the economy each year through increased crime: $170 billion
- Estimated amount they cost the US economy through higher health care costs: $160 billion
- % of GOP House & Senate members in an April, 2006 poll who believed humans cause climate change: 23
- % who believed this in January, 2007: 16

—*Harper's Magazine Index*, April, 2007

How crazy is America? An impossible-imponderable question, no doubt (how to quantify the problems of millions of people with dysfunctional brains in a society both dully conformist and chaotically centrifugal?); but all the evidence says: on the whole, mighty loco. We put hundreds of thousands of people in prison for making, using, or selling the drugs we damn, while we bless the manufacture, use, and sale of other drugs, some of which, like nicotine, are known to be lethal. We laud ourselves as the world's great peacemaker (and extirpator of WMDs) while stockpiling enough such weapons to incinerate the world hundreds of times over. We fan ourselves into hysteria over rumors of being attacked by terrorists, while attacking other countries for no good reason.

We're a spectacularly obese nation that worships thinness. Having exploited, degraded, and all but destroyed the land's original human inhabitants (along with other native species), we mythicize and romanticize them in movies and every conceivable iconographic venue, from coins to postage stamps to team names (now frowned on by the NCAA) . We bewail our dependence on foreign oil while proudly driving around in bloated gas-guzzlers.

The two institutions we idolize above all others are health care and education. So we spend hundreds of billions of dollars mis-treating the nation (even insured Americans, with the most expensive health care in the world, aren't healthy) and mis-educating our youth (who bring up the rear in most subjects worldwide). We have a health care system where more people are pushing paper than healing bodies. We glamorize doctors, and then sue them for millions if we're not completely satisfied with their services.

We have thousands of colleges and universities (nearly 4,000), the bulk of which will take practically any applicant who can afford to pay, and where students can pursue such lofty disciplines as recreation and leisure studies, sports marketing, concrete management [i.e., how to manage concrete], landscaping, apparel merchandising, etc. To drive away the boredom inevitably accompanying, if not stifling, college life, students can always go to watch their semi-professional "student-athlete" classmates play in huge stadiums or courts (aka "facilities"), with the best training that millionaire-coaches and de luxe equipment rooms can provide. (See Chapter 14, "What We're Really Good At.")

If nothing else, American college sports—which have no parallel anywhere else on the planet—provide an excellent boot camp for the pros. For the countless jocks who neither graduate nor make it as professionals, the whole experience will presumably at least remain as a brief, sweet sojourn in the mythical American field of dreams. As for the graduates, athletes or otherwise, they'll be ready to tackle almost every imaginable field of endeavor, although 42% of them will never read a book again.

If they find the quality of primary and secondary education isn't low enough for them, Americans can always venture into the foggy nether regions of home-schooling, where as of 2008 there seem to be something over two million children (about the same, coincidentally, as the number of adults in prison), and where parents, most of them religious fanatics, try to shield their offspring from the various contaminants of public life.

Fortunately, there are enough bright and industrious East Asians, South Asians, Jews and geeks of every description to provide a clerisy to deal with the nation's needs.

In any event, the whole crazy expanse of American life is awash in semi-laughable contradictions. We 're totally fixated on breasts (something over a quarter-million surgical implants performed every year—what "personal make-over" would be complete without one?), and deluge our cultural space with every conceivable form of luscious cleavage and decolletage; but then have moral apoplexy over Janet Jackson's wardrobe malfunction. (Congresswoman Heather Wilson of New Mexico, a Ph.D. and a member of the League of Conservation Voters' Dirty Dozen, openly wept over this life-altering, traumatic episode on national TV. "You knew what you were doing," she righteously lashed out at the president of Viacom. "You knew what kind of entertainment you're selling, and you wanted us all to be abuzz, here in this room and on the playground and in my kids' school, because it improves your ratings.") And millions of Americans cheered her. Virtuous Congresspeople immediately moved to raise the penalties on rampant lustfulness in the media.

We're bonkers about pets (88 million cats? 75 million dogs?), as a stroll down the pet-food and pet-supplies aisle in any supermarket will verify. But we have no problem with slaughtering nine billion or so birds and beasts every year, mostly under horrific conditions after utterly miserable lives. We sentimentalize and brutalize animals in roughly equal measure. Stuffed toys, soppy movies (*Happy Feet, Homeward Bound, The Adventures of Milo and Otis, Free Willy*), and tortured veal calves, chickens, pigs, etc. Michael Vick gets 23 months in the slammer for killing dogs, while fur is ever so popular (check the fashion mags and the pronouncements of pelt-loving gurus like Anna Wintour).

And finally there's the age-old clash between the ideal of equality and the fact of plutocracy. Is our era of wretched excess worse than the Gilded Age? Are today's corporate criminals, the Ken Lays, and Bernie Ebberses, and Dennis Kozlowskis, any different from the robber barons? Do our most porcine capitalists, for instance UnitedHealth's William W. McGuire (that's *Doctor* McGuire to you), Home Depot's Robert Nardelli,or the NYSEC's Richard Grasso, deserve any specially high level of obloquy after all we've seen from the other captains of industry? Who can say? One thing for sure: we're better informed about the shenanigans of the mega-rich than we used to be. We know how long their yachts are, how broad their golden parachutes, what silly $10,000 Christmas presents they buy their pets; and so contemporary populists—armed with data from reporters like *The New York Times*' Gretchen Morgenson or *The Wall Street Journal*'s Robert Frank—can enjoy an open season on the fat cats, even while the breed increases, multiplies, and flourishes. And some day, who knows, *we* might end up in their exalted company—it's the updated American Dream (former bad boy Dennis Hopper swears so on TV).

That spectacle, of course, makes an awkward contrast with the 36 million or so Americans living below the federal poverty line, the 38 million or so "food-insecure" Americans, the 47 million or so Americans with no health insurance, and all the millions inhabiting the various preserves of misery across the land: the ghettoized underclass, the illegal immigrants, the homeless, the unemployed, the fruit and vegetable pickers, the meat-packing proletariat, etc. But nobody likes cognitive dissonance, so we avoid it by ignoring all the wretches (poverty, as opposed to picturesque disasters, doesn't qualify as "news"*) and turning the criminal "lifestyles of the rich and famous" into a source of voyeuristic (pseudo-)mocking amusement. As Peter Singer has pointed out, we view all contributions, however small, by all plutocrats, however stingy, as admirable acts of virtue (and hence tax deductible). Singer's notion that anyone who could easily remedy other people's suffering and doesn't is guilty of prolonging it strikes Americans as utopian do-goodery (just check the statistics in "What Should a Billionaire Give—And What Should You?")

But this sort of flight from reality and escape into irrational thinking is just your basic American schizophrenia (you mean reality TV isn't real?)—or about what one would expect from the inhabitants of Loonyland.

---

* Kudos to John Seigenthaler for his bucking this trend with his ongoing, in-depth reports on MSNBC about life in American prisons.

Chapter 3

Scoundrels Swarming in the Last Refuge

THE PRESIDENT: Thank you all. (Applause.) Mr. Chairman—Mr. Chairman, delegates, fellow citizens: I am honored by your support, and I accept your nomination for President of the United States. (Applause.) When I—when I said those words four years ago, none of us could have envisioned what these years would bring. In the heart of this great city, we saw tragedy arrive on a quiet morning. We saw the bravery of rescuers grow with danger. We learned of passengers on a doomed plane who died with a courage that frightened their killers. (Applause.) We have seen a shaken economy rise to its feet. And we have seen Americans in uniform storming mountain strongholds, and charging through sandstorms, and liberating millions, with acts of valor that would make the men of Normandy proud. (Applause.)

Since 2001, Americans have been given hills to climb, and found the strength to climb them. Now, because we have made the hard journey, we can see the valley below. Now, because we have faced challenges with resolve, we have historic goals within our reach, and greatness in our future. We will build a safer world and a more hopeful America—and nothing will hold us back. (Applause.)

In the work we have done, and the work we will do, I am fortunate to have a superb Vice President. (Applause.) I have counted on Dick Cheney's calm and steady judgment in difficult days, and I am honored to have him at my side. (Applause.)

—George W. Bush, September 2, 2004

9/11 unleashed, among other things, a toxic tidal wave of patriotism that seems likely to poison this country for years to come, if not for the rest of our lives. All the WTC victims were immediately acclaimed as "heroes," as were, and still are, all members of the Armed Forces sent to die amid the futile horror of the war in Iraq. (Alas, the "hero" badge wasn't awarded retroactively to those who died in the Oklahoma City or the first WTC bombings, perhaps for financial reasons.) The political skies are now full of chicken hawks, from paunchy neo-cons to veteran draft-dodgers like Bush and Cheney to freshman Congresspeople like Jean Schmidt of Ohio, who achieved her one and only moment of fame by accusing John Murtha of cowardice. Police-state spying and entrapment of clueless "home-grown" plotters are flourishing, while skeptical press reports about them are labeled as treason. The non-existent menace of flag-burning-and-desecration is widely deplored.

And, best of all, we now have a magical new category of evil, "terrorism," with its endless host of comic-book villains, the "terrorists" (ideally pronounced as a two-syllable word). Inventing the "terr'rists," one has to admit, was a stroke of genius. Unlike normal adversaries, terr'rists are completely irrational. In their dark, primitive way they "hate our freedoms," i.e., every noble thing we stand for, and by definition show no mercy, restraint, or logic in assaulting their innocent victims. Hence, they can be dealt with only as we deal with mad dogs, poisonous snakes or cancer—by relentless annihilation. The mantra of "terr'rism" can be rendered even more powerful by linking it with the fearful and always authentic-sounding adjective "al-Qaeda." Granted, "al-Qaeda" operatives make up only a small part of the worldwide militia that hates our freedoms (and there was no al-Qaeda in Iraq till Operation Iraqi Freedom installed it), so overusing the term may ultimately backfire by aggrandizing this especially obnoxious group—only to remind people that despite Bush's macho swagger, Osama Bin Laden remains at large, calmly thumbing his proverbial nose at his sworn enemy.

The terrorists' continued survival (and their ready replaceability when killed) is the bad news; the good news is that by their very nature, these diabolical fiends confirm our essential goodness. And, unlike other enemies, they can never be finally defeated, so they'll always be around as a permanent excuse for extracurricular smears, vendettas, crack-downs, and ideological orgies of any sort. An improved version of Cavafy's barbarians, they serve as a sort of ultimate solution.

Welcome to the Age of Patriotism. But what will this mean, beyond the proliferation of flags waving in front yards or attached to car radio antennas or gymnasium floors or the uniforms of high school-college-or-pro athletes, of "I support our troops" bumper stickers, and red-white-and-blue decals everywhere? Right-wing talk show ranters and red state fear-mongers will now never need to shut up. Left-wing satirists will have targets aplenty. The USA Patriot Act will, of course, be renewed ad infinitum, since anyone opposed to it would by definition be aiding and abetting the Powers of Darkness. Given that, unlike flesh-and-blood enemies, terror is a method, and a more or less immortal one, from here on in the War on Terror will never end , i.e., we'll live in the permanent state of emergency that tyrants have dreamed of and created whenever they could.

Beyond all that, it's no surprise to see the religion of national self-worship bloom as never before. Faith needs persecution, or at least anxiety-ridden confrontation (recall the recent laughable protests against the "war on Christmas"), to prosper; and the sources of anxiety are now close to infinite. *Everything* in the country from nuclear power plants to petting zoos has been officially certified as vulnerable to attack: our harbors, our transportation system, our public buildings, our subways, tunnels, and schools, our communication networks, our air, water, and food supply. Cold-war Communists were a distant fantasy, ICBMs from the USSR or China were more like science fiction; but *this* is the real deal. The supply of angry Muslims will never dry up (our own policies help to insure that); so we can never, ever lay our guard down. This war will the longest one in our history (to the permanent delight of jingoists and the military-industrial complex) Strategies and tactics on both sides will evolve endlessly, as the virus of terrorism mutates in resistance to our endless efforts to kill it once and for all. Who could ask for anything more?

Certainly not our scoundrels: heartland demagogues, fascist bloggers, rabid televangelists, NASCAR Republicans, Ann Coulter fans, or red-blooded good old boys like former Rep. John Cooksey (R-Louisiana), who issued the famous Helpful Hint for Catching Terrorists, "If I hear someone come in and he's got a diaper on his head and a fan belt around that diaper on his head, that guy needs to be pulled over and checked." *À la guerre, comme à la guerre*, as some of Cooksey's old constituents might have said.

Everyone acknowledges—well, countless writers have agreed—that in wartime the first casualty is truth. And how not? We may be angry, for example, that the stories of Jessica Lynch and Pat Tilman were falsified by the Army for propaganda; but we can hardly be surprised. The problem is not that the War on Terrorism has spawned an extraordinary number of lies; but that since it has no expiration date, we may have to get used to living in a permanent fog of mendacity. We've already seen quite of lot of that at White House press conferences, as well as from the Pentagon, the CIA, and the State department, for the past six years or so.

Then too, people who've been attacked (and who believe they may be attacked again) may well become paranoid; and paranoid individuals will do things like tap your phones, scan your bank records, check what books you've borrowed from the library, and maybe even arrest you without charges and hold you incommunicado. Stuff happens.

But, no matter how bad things get—and even patriots sometimes find airport security a pain in the neck—we'll always be the greatest country in the world: the land that fought a glorious and perfectly unnecessary Revolutionary War (ditto for the pointless War of 1812, the land-grabbing Mexican War, the fratricidal-suicidal Civil War, the gangsterish Spanish-American War, the worse-than-useless First World War, which made the Second one inevitable, the catastrophic Vietnam War, the brainless Bushie Iraq War . . .), that exploited millions of black slaves, that slaughtered millions of Indians, annihilated much of its wildlife, devastated its environment, created a culture of towering banality and intoxicated wastefulness—I mean, it doesn't get much better than this, does it? My country 'tis of thee. . . . We're all patriots now: members of Congress have to wear American flag pins in their lapels or on their dresses (lest they be mistaken for suicide-vested aliens). Professional athletes (and refs) likewise have to flaunt the Stars and Stripes on their shirts, caps, helmets, whatever. Fans at Yankee Stadium have to take time out during the seventh inning stretch to "honor America. Newark airport has been rebaptized Newark Liberty airport. And political hopefuls now make all their campaign appearances against a humongous backdrop blanket of Red, White, and Blue.

Meanwhile, nobody dares say the simple truth that for most practical purposes patriotism is just egoism writ large, a kind of masturbatory ritual where you needn't feel ashamed of pleasuring yourself in public since so many other people are doing the same. Now there's a thought: vocal patriots as circle-jerkers. Unfortunately, the Jeffersonian tree of liberty is supposed to be refreshed ("from time to time," as he said) with the *blood* of patriots, not their idly scattered seed, which only leaves behind an icky adolescent mess.

Chapter 4

A Nation of Make-Believers

Then the preacher begun to preach, and begun in earnest, too; and went weaving first to one side of the platform and then the other, and then a-leaning down over the front of it, with his arms and his body going all the time, and shouting his words out with all his might; and every now and then he would hold up his Bible and spread it open, and kind of pass it around this way and that, shouting, "It's the brazen serpent in the wilderness! Look upon it and live!" And people would shout out, "Glory!—A-a-MEN!" And so he went on, and the people groaning and crying and saying amen:

"Oh, come to the mourners' bench! come, black with sin! (AMEN!) come, sick and sore! (AMEN!) come, lame and halt and blind! (AMEN!) come, pore and needy, sunk in shame! (A-A-MEN!) come, all that's worn and soiled and suffering!—come with a broken spirit! come with a contrite heart! come in your rags and sin and dirt! the waters that cleanse is free, the door of heaven stands open—oh, enter in and be at rest!" (A-A-MEN! GLORY, GLORY HALLELUJAH!)

And so on. You couldn't make out what the preacher said any more, on account of the shouting and crying. Folks got up everywheres in the crowd, and worked their way just by main strength to the mourners' bench, with the tears running down their faces; and when all the mourners had got up there to the front benches in a crowd, they sung and shouted and flung themselves down on the straw, just crazy and wild.

—*The Adventures of Huckleberry Finn*, Chapter 20

Even though Jews make up only about 2% of America's population, the vast majority of their fellow citizens seem to have lined up behind the nameless rabbi in I. B. Singer's *Gimpel the Fool* who said that believing is good for you—never mind the odds of its being true. Americans are the faith-full outliers in an increasingly skeptical First World, with 85-90% regularly proclaiming their belief in God and related traditional ideas. It's hard to imagine any other country whipping up the sort of collective fanaticism and phoniness on display, for example, in that latter-day revival of Huckleberry Finn's prayer meeting, *Jesus Camp*.

A massive recent (Sept. 2006) study, *American Piety in the 21st Century*, by a research group at Baylor (with polling by Gallup) confirms and expands on this pattern of credulity. For example, even though nearly 11% of the sample group were not affiliated with any church, congregation or religious group (meaning, of course that nine out of ten Americans *did* so belong), about 60% of the *unaffiliated* folks believe in God (or a "higher power") anyway. 11% believe that Jesus is the Son of God, and a whopping 10% pray at least once a day. So much for unbelief.

Among the card-carrying Christians, naturally, the numbers are much richer. Almost half of the 100 million Evangelicals are biblical literalists (God said it, I believe it, that settles it). Nearly half (44%) of American Christians have seen *The Passion of the Christ*—and presumably loved it. Americans buy millions of books from the *Left-Behind* series, along with the works of the revolting James Dobson and the rather more decent Rick Warren.

Black Protestants (100% of whom claim to have no doubts whatsoever that God exists) and Evangelical Protestants overwhelmingly (ca. 95%) believe that Jesus is the son of God—whatever that means. Two-thirds to three-quarters of the same twin group pray once or more every day; and about half of them go to services every week. This fervor cools when we shift our focus to mainline Protestants and Roman Catholics, while Jews in general set a sorry example of scraping-the-bottom religiosity, with only 9% believing that the Bible is literally true. Well, that's their lookout.

The long and the short of it is that Americans are brainlessly addicted to religion; and those who aren't try to hide the fact. (The aptly named Congressman Pete Stark of California made headlines in March, 2007 by coming out as an atheist, the first lawmaker to do so in something like all of recorded history. A tiny handful of other Capitol Hill freethinkers report their religious affiliation as "Not Stated," which in

God-awful America translates as something close to bomb-throwing radical). Americans believe in creation rather than evolution (while maintaining that, for the sake of fairness, both should be taught in the public schools), in the Virgin Birth, in miracles of every sort, in the sacred-sadistic prophecies from the Book of Revelation (coming soon to a planet near you), and, above all, in their own prospects for happy-ever-aftering in heaven.

Their faith makes them support the death penalty, condemn abortion, fret about stem-cell research, insist on the "under God" addendum to the Pledge of Allegiance, and want to post the Ten Commandments in schools and courthouses. Americans flock to mega-churches, wear crosses around their necks, tattoo them on their arms, and dangle them over their dashboards. They slaughter and devour tens of millions of turkeys by way of thanking Jehovah, decry homosexuality in general and gay marriage in particular, and send their children to schools with names like Notre Dame, Southern Methodist, Texas Christian, Brigham Young, Oral Roberts, and Liberty University (where intellectual liberty is severely constrained). They vote for politicians who flaunt their piety, like George "Jesus-is-my-favorite-philosopher" Bush, Oklahoma Senator James Inhofe (who believes in the Resurrection, but not global warming), and Rep. Chip Pickering from the Third District in Mississippi, who can be seen leading a noisy but transparently phony Jesus-screaming orgy in *Borat*. They festoon their cars with bumper stickers with cutely pious quips like, "Christians aren't perfect . . . just forgiven" or "My boss is a Jewish carpenter" or "In case of rapture this car will be unmanned." They're on God's side—but, hey, who isn't?

Mountains of books have been written to explain and analyze and warn about such things; and while no one person could claim to be on top of all the (generally depressing) data, their drift is clear: this country was founded by independent-minded religious fanatics, who left a deep mark behind them. It underwent a tumultuous series of 19th century religious revivals, with some 20th century aftershocks. Its lack of an established church has helped reduce, if not eliminate, European-style anticlericalism. Its pragmatic anti-intellectual mind-set has welcomed all sorts of homemade, half-baked, eccentric creeds, like the Mormons, Christian Scientists, Pentecostalists, and Seventh Day Adventists.

America's nearly unlimited tolerance for theism in its myriad shapes and guises has flung open the gates to an army of uncritical *croyants*, who may not—and do not—know much about science, history, or philosophy, but who share a rock-solid confidence in such mystical tenets as: I. Everything happens for a reason (consider the terrifying nihilistic-common sense alternative); II. Someone in the Great Somewhere hears every word (are you kidding?); III. Prayer works wonders (or at least can't hurt—in fact, when, in the entire course of human history, has praying ever done the slightest bit of harm?); IV. Jesus saves (or at least helps an awful lot); V. Heaven is real-even-if-indescribable (and patriarchal families play a huge part in it, just ask the Mormons); VI. God has a Definite Set of Rules (and we all pretty much know what they are, though you can look them up in the Bible, if you've gotten a little rusty); and, of course, VII. Atheists can't be trusted (with your kids, your money, your government, anything).

None of the foregoing Divine Dictates can stand up to serious questioning; but they don't have to. Americans have by and large agreed to take them on faith—let the handful of snotty God-deniers-in-disguise at Americans United (or even up-front atheistic jokesters like Phil Maher or Stephen Colbert or—yipes—Penn and Teller) carp away as much as they like.

There's no point arguing with the religionists, because they're not interested in reasons or susceptible to reasoning. (That would be Tenet VIII: Logic can get you only so far; at some point you *have to* take a leap of faith (life is a high dive or, at the least, a hurdles-event). Or, more elegantly (violins, please) *Le coeur a ses raisons que la raison ne connaît point*. So God, who manufactured and micro-manages creation, sends magical messages down to a mysteriously chosen in-crowd. People have souls, and animals don't, which is why *we* all live forever and they don't. Eternal punishment is not only conceivable, but (in some cases anyhow) richly deserved. A murdered preacher saved the world, nay the entire universe, with a few liters of his precious blood (shed in the course of particularly painful afternoon). Miracles can happen, actually they have never stopped happening, as any number of true-life testimonials in *Reader's Digest* and elsewhere demonstrate. The sky's the limit.

In the end, as everyone knows, the opposite of love isn't hate, it's indifference. Brainless American piety has to be classified as a bizarre love-disease (if we discount the millions of palpable phonies and knee-jerk believers). Our make-believers think they're in love; and it'll take wave after wave of chilly indifference to cure it. These will issue forth from the usual mental and psychic regions: education, scientific and otherwise, critical reading of the Bible, disappointment with religion's blind spots (e.g., the rights of women and non-human nature) unkept promises (the increasingly obvious non-existence of the afterlife), and spreading awareness that God isn't needed (is in fact an obstacle) if you want to fashion an intellectually and emotionally satisfying moral code. Then, for as much of world history is left before humanity destroys the planet, a nation of believers could turn into a nation of more or less *non*-deranged humans. Of course, that would be a very different country from the America we know.

Chapter 5

Natural Splendor, National Squalor

> We are the nation of human progress, and who will, what can, set limits to our onward march?
>
> —John L. O'Sullivan, The Democratic Review (1839)

> Our national flower is the concrete cloverleaf.
>
> —Lewis Mumford, Quote Magazine (1961)

Gatlinburg, Tennessee; Estes Park, Colorado; Tusayan, Arizona; Springdale, Utah. The names probably don't ring any, or many, bells, but they're all towns lying just outside four of our greatest national parks. They all live off the tourist trade, and they're all really ugly, with strings of motels, gas stations, mini-marts, curio shops, laundromats, etc., scattered hither and yon, their neon or plastic signs clamoring for the motorist's attention. Of course, passing vacationers are happy to use their services; and, however helter-skelter or dismal their appearance, they're doubtless no worse than most other dismal samples of American highway architecture, the Strip.

The problem is, they contrast so joltingly with the natural beauty all around them, with the splendors of the Smokies, the Rockies, the Grand Canyon, or Zion National Park. They remind us too pointedly of William Cowper's tag that "God made the country, and man made the town." This is especially striking in the Southwest, because not very far from the hideous sprawl of places like Phoenix, Flagstaff, and Albuquerque, we find very different sorts of "towns": haunting Anasazi ruins like those at Mesa Verde, Betatakin, or Walnut Canyon (not to mention a few still functioning pueblos like Taos or Acoma), which blend into the surrounding desert with unassuming grace. The Indian cliff dwellings offer a thoughtful integration of humans and nature, while our squalid tract housing and trailer parks suggest a state of war.

As any trip to the West reminds us, Americans are in many ways still living on the frontier. There's the nomadism (monthly warehouse rentals for the working class, Winnebagos for the bourgeoisie, Jackson Hole chalets for the upper crust), the violence (the bullet-ridden road signs all over the Mountain West, the ubiquitous guns, the dozens of towns whose names begin with "Fort"), and the restless haste (fast food, fast driving, mushrooming construction) we associate with the 19th century pioneers. This life has its sort-of charms—the wide open, come-as-you-are, sky's-the-limit ethos—but it also has its hideous price, as seen in the yawning mindlessness of Sun Belt cities, the Amarillos and Tulsas and Tucsons. Like the mountain men who first explored the West (of whom only an estimated 5% worked as trappers until retirement), too many Americans are in a hurry to make a killing and move on. George Santayana's dictum that no American lives where he was born or believes what he was taught is as close to the truth as ever. The staggering stone shapes of Yosemite Valley and Zion Canyon took millions of years to evolve, while the towns around them—and much of the U.S.A.—grew up overnight, under fierce economic pressure and with predictabley grungy results.

And so we have the familiar paradox that America combines the most varied and dramatic landscapes in the world (from the Adirondacks to the Everglades to the Tetons to Death Valley to the Sierras and on and on) with the most banal urban scenery (fill in your candidate for Supremely Boring Burg—Terre Haute? Joplin? Lubbock? Logan? Fresno?) anywhere. There are streets in Italy (the Grand Canal in Venice, the Via del Corso in Rome) with more esthetic and historical interest than the entire city of Los Angeles, not to say all the conurbations of the state of California. But then Rome was notoriously not built in a day, and what have the Italians done to their wilderness?

Our culture needs time—the question is, will we get it? It doesn't look good at the moment—to heal, to mellow, to mature. We're a nation of newly rich kids (rich partly because we're workaholics, but mostly because of the fabulous natural resources we stumbled on, stole, and exploited); and so we're the kind of people who tend to be crude, short-sighted, and wasteful. Again, look at the frontier: in less than 20 years (mid-1820's to early 1840's) the mountain men swept from New Mexico to California, "leaving behind them," in the words of historian Ray Allen

Billington, "a land so ruthlessly overtrapped that beaver were virtually exterminated." Many Forty Niners pulled up stakes from the Mother Lode country after a few years and sped off on gold rushes to Idaho, British Columbia, Nevada, Arizona, and Colorado.

Today's ghost towns and abandoned mine sites testify to their ephemeral but destructive presence. First, the Sooners wiped out the Indians (all along US Highway 40 you'll find commemorative plaques about the tribes formerly inhabiting the sites). Then wrong-headed farming methods helped create the Dust Bowl. By 1938 something like 28% of Oklahoma's farm population (275,000 people) had moved to a new farm the year before. "Within a single generation," writes Professor Donald Worster," [the Okies'] last frontier had already become a rural slum."

Life on the frontier was a messy business. Crossing Nevada in 1862, Mark Twain observed that "the road was white with the bones of oxen and horses. . . . The desert was one prodigious graveyard. And the log chains, wagon tires, and rotting wrecks of vehicles were almost as thick as the bones."

A century and a half ago Twain was exhilarated by the wild freedom of the stagecoach ride from St. Joseph to Carson City; he was thrilled by Lake Tahoe ("the fairest picture the whole earth affords"). But he was disgusted by the casual bloodshed in Virginia City, and he described the universal "silver fever" as insane. We had then, as we have now, what looks like the most beautiful country in the world, the most spectacular assemblage of mountains, deserts, prairies, and forests anywhere, but were we ready for it? Are we ready for it now? Nope—judging from what we did inside and outside the Everglades (now less half their original size, with all sorts of damage to original species there—for the sake of the South Florida's cancerous "civilization"—see Carl Hiaasen's Paradise Screwed), practically all of Hawaii (catastrophic assault on the rain forests, introduction of lethal alien species), and the devastation radiating out from the center of America's New Zion, Las Vegas, including the drowned Glen Canyon and the idiotic Lake Mead (currently at less than half capacity and doomed to slowly evaporate in the desert).

Adam and Eve's extremely minor bit of bad behavior (they were just trying to find out what it meant to be grown-ups) got them expelled from Eden. But a defenseless naked couple were a piece of cake to handle. Now God himself couldn't drive their uppity 300-plus million American descendants out of the garden they've trashed. We've got a lock on the joint. Too bad.

Chapter 6

Throwing Our Weight Around

> The visionary engineer Paul MacCready has made an arresting calculation: ten thousand years ago, human beings (plus their domestic animals) accounted for less than a tenth of 1 percent (by weight) of all vertebrate life on earth and in the air. Back then we were just another mammalian species and not a particularly populous one (he estimates eighty million people worldwide). Today, that percentage, including livestock and pets, is in the neighborhood of 98!
>
> —Daniel C. Dennett, *Breaking the Spell* (2006)

Nature, as Bill McKibben pointed out back in 1989, is effectively passé. Earth has been so human-ized, so shaped and stamped and stomped by the things we've done and are doing to it that it barely resembles what emerged from the imagined hands or breath of its Creator. For example, you can't drink unfiltered water anywhere in the lower 48 states, even in the "wilderness," without risking giardiasis—one of the vilest forms of diarrhea ever devised, but an exquisitely karmic metaphor of shit producing more shit. Environmental degradation of every sort—deforestation, desertification, destruction of animals and their habitat, pollution of land, water, and air, global warming, overpopulation (till recently by everyone, now mostly by the poor), lunatic over-consumption by the rich, you name it—has turned the world into a string of giant graffiti: Kilroy Was Here.

This is, of course, by definition a planetary problem. (Or maybe not so much a problem—since that tame word implies a solution; and there's a very good chance that, even if a solution exists, it'll be ignored, and we'll all go under—as a condition, and a terminal condition at that.) But the American version of the problem has a unique face, a uniquely bloated and banal and self-congratulatory/self-exculpatory look, something like a glossy SUV ad with a squeaky-clean young family gazing beatifically out over the Grand Canyon at sunset, the latest generation off to see the USA (America's the greatest land of all!) in their Chevrolet or whatever. This land *is*, after all, *our* land, isn't it—you know, like, from California to the New York Island, from the red wood forests to the Gulf stream wa-a-a-ters. This land was made for you and me and the rest of our 300-plus million horde. Which is why we're here.

In fact, a Martian watching some TV ads might get the impression that much—or most—of the US was still beautiful virgin territory or, as we like to say, untamed wilderness, a giant circle of interconnected national parks. And there is, to be sure, a tiny grain of truth in that picturesque fantasy. Compared with pullulating Europe or Asia, America *is* less densely populated and has more wide-open spaces. A few years ago a colleague of mine was driving some Israeli friends through the Adirondack Mountains (a 6.1 million acre state park) on the Northway, when one of them enviously scanned the horizon and remarked, "*Ze lo fair*"—this isn't fair. Scrunched into their tiny, conflicted, and overpopulated country, Israelis quite naturally marveled at the thought of having so much wide-open territory. But that's just because the technology-laden, heedlessly breeding white invaders didn't arrive in considerable numbers until the 19th century—after which they moved fast and furiously (as the Brazilians began to do a century later). It takes time to engulf the place—but we're catching up.

By now we're all hunkered down in the Paradise parking lot, witnesses to the devolutionary panorama of Robert Crumb's "Short History of America." But the "problem" isn't simply with the strip malls, strip mines, and superhighways linking one soulless inner city to another, the numbing suburbs, factory farms, fast food joints, dollar stores, oxymoronic industrial parks, garbage dumps, junk-yards, land-fills, and so on—that is, not just with their throwaway ugliness or infectious desolation. It's the human-all-too-humanness—in our case you could call it, for lack of a better word, Americanness. We broke it (with God's blessing), and we own it.

Maybe great architecture—of which we have so little, and that little scattered hither and yon—can lift us up into some higher realm; but the stuff *we*'ve got, after uprooting, bulldozing, and reshaping, traps us deeper inside the dullest part of ourselves. Again, this is to some degree a familiar refrain, as in Hopkins' "God's Grandeur":

> Generations have trod, have trod, have trod;
> And all is seared with trade; bleared, smeared with toil;
> And wears man's smudge and shares man's smell: The soil
> Is bare now, nor can foot feel, being shod.

That state of affairs obviously obtained in Victorian England and obtains now, for example, in the industrial waste land of the former Second World, in places like Poland and Hungary, where statues left outdoors crumble in the poisoned air. Even the minimal environmental protection that US law requires costs a lot of money; and poor countries can't spare it, as they spin forward into capitalist toxicity. Woe betide the Chinese.

But what seems to mark the technically milder American way of crushing nature is the smiley-faces painted all over it, pretending that the mine-pit is a sandbox, that the snake-pit is a petting zoo. Destroying is transmogrified into "developing." Raping the Arctic National Wildlife Refuge is pitched as a purely patriotic act, aimed at (though guaranteed never to achieve, or even to help achieve) "energy independence" and God knows what other kinds of rugged American individuality. (Cf. Mount Rushmore, Stone Mountain, and similar self-centered national mega-monstrosities.) Wal-Mart, all crude facts to the contrary, pictures itself as a vast welfare operation, selflessly seeking out communities in distress and rescuing poor wretches with a combination of fabulously fulfilling jobs as "associates" and spectacularly discounted prices for stuff that W-M's corporate serfs may, if they're lucky, be able to buy.

We relentlessly sentimentalize our semi-ruined landscapes. All the dead stretches of New York disappear in Woody Allen's *Manhattan* and *Friends* (the city as playground for the idle bourgeoisie). Even the supposedly gritty urban jungle of *NYPD* is more colorful and cool than grim and desperate. West Virginia? Sweeping vistas of high green hills, with John Denver gently begging those practically deserted country roads to "take me home." Forget about the mountain-tops (the "overburden") blasted to kingdom come, chemically enriched rivers, silicosis, etc. California? Let's see, that would be *Baywatch* beaches, lavish McMansions (even the Fresh Prince got one) dreaming in the sun, picturesque Chicanos laughing while their adorable kids whack away at piñatas, white picket-fence suburbia, temple-garages everywhere, the greensward gleaming with acid rain and perky little yellow flags warning that the ChemLawn truck has just been through, and you really don't want to go anywhere near the stuff they've pumped into the soil.

What's missing from this picture? Duh—feed-lots, stockyards, meat-packing plants (abattoirs), pig-farm sewage, rush-hour traffic jams, armies of sedentary fat people waddling through overstocked supermarkets (the Dept. of Agriculture says Americans waste 96 billion pounds of food a year), millions of mindless humans cheering NASCAR events, acres of phone-banks, computer screens, and keyboards, attached to endless rows of mildly-to-severely bored slaves, metastasized metropolises (though admittedly less hideous than the slums of, say, Lagos, Cairo, Mexico City, São Paulo, Calcutta, or Baghdad), the whole sorry spectacle of nature re-created by humans.

What a lovely mirror-image. When you're as fat as we are (*Epidemiologic Reviews* estimates that within a few years (2015), 75% of Americans will be overweight and a rollicking 48% will be obese), when your bodies and the ludicrously huge life-support system we've plugged them into spin out of control, the ground trembles beneath your feet. When you're the biggest (if not smartest) kid on the block, you've got to throw your weight around. And, man, do we ever.

Chapter 7

Wait, There's More!

> Americans constitute 5% of the world's population, but consume 24% of the world's energy. On average, one American consumes as much energy as 2 Japanese, 6 Mexicans, 13 Chinese. 31 Indians, 128 Bangladeshis, 307 Tanzanians, and 370 Ethiopians. Americans eat 815 billion calories of food each day, roughly 200 billion more than needed, enough to feed 80 million people, Americans throw out 200,000 tons of food daily. The average American generates 52 tons of garbage by age 75.
>
> —www.mindfully.org/Sustainability/
> American-Consume-24percent.htm

The problem with America is not simply that there's too much of everything—in which case redistribution, unlikely as that would be, might solve our problems—but that amid the insane proliferation of things—in malls and halls, on shelves, streets and electronic screens, in closets and drawers, in basements and attics, in our bodies and brains—so much of the stuff is crap (see Chapter 12, "It's Offal, It's Awful, It's All We've Got"), and just having it or being around it is unhealthy.

In itself, sheer abundance, the vast avalanche of things advertised—and available! now!—on the Home Shopping Network, in a trillion TV and radio commercials, newspaper supplements, mail order catalogs, and junk mailings—mightn't be so bad. You could take a Wall Street Journal view of it as the exuberant self-expression of the world's largest free market: hundreds of millions of producers and consumers buying and selling with awesome energy and huge resources, wildly fluctuating standards of taste, and (thank goodness) no totalitarian government to dictate our choices.

It does, often enough, make for a gaudy show, from the floor of the New York Stock Exchange to neighborhood garage sales, from Neiman Marcus to Wal-Mart, from Christie's to eBay, from L.L. Bean's to Victoria's Secret. Who could count all cars in California, the motor boats in Florida, the slot machines in Nevada, the fast food joints and gas stations flanking Interstate 40 or 90, and, best of all (well, maybe not), the web sites on the Internet? Has there ever been—anywhere in the world, at any time in world history—a dazzling cornucopia to match any really big contemporary America supermarket?

But take a closer look at the hypoquality of this hyperquantity, and problems positively erupt. Given the unmanageable dimensions of this American mess, the best way to scan it may be with a non-methodical list. We have too too much of:

1. WMDs (nuclear warheads, Star Wars missile destroyers, bombs of every kind)
2. Billionaires and millionaires (CEO salaries, plutocratic tax breaks)
3. Bad chemicals (alcohol, nicotine, drugs, sugar, salt, additives)
4. Food (fats to the fat, meat [almost a pound a day in the USA])
5. People without health insurance (permanently or occasionally)
6. "News" (celebritology, weather reports)
7. "Entertainment" (game shows, sit-coms, reality TV, Las Vegas)
8. Paved-over space (parking lots)
9. Guns (280 million or so)
10. Work (24/7)
11. Noise (traffic, p.a. systems, chainsaws, lawnmowers, jingling ice cream trucks)
12. Pets (we love cats, dogs, and birds, but butcher, cows, pigs, and chickens)
13. Religion (televangelists, mega-churches, Christian posturing by politicians)
14. Sports (seasons too long, players too drugged, games too hyped)
15. Packaging (cardboard boxes, shrink wrap, paper and plastic bags)
16. Debt (credit card and otherwise, unpayable mortgages, etc.)
17. Books, DVDs (self-help! horror! romance! sex!)

18. Toys, gadgets, hardware, home-improvement paraphernalia.
19. Election campaigns (followed inch by inch by the commentariat-lemmings)
20. Literal garbage (the incalculable mass of our dumpsters and landfills)

And on it goes: too little of what we need, too much of what we don't. What an awe-inspiring array of dreck. Bourgeois weddings are too vulgar and expensive (quite apart from the fact that they don't "take"). Restaurant portions are too big. There are too many brands—of everything from household cleansers to electronic products. The Sunday Times is too bulky (down crash our forests). The gap between the rich—stockbrokers, hedge fund managers, rock stars, and fashion designers. among others—and the poor is way too wide and growing wider. (Let Lou Dobbs weep for the forgotten middle class; the truly forgotten Americans are the underclass). Detroit's cars, too large and too thirsty, come with too many useless options. There are too many cartoons, game shows, soap operas, and inane sit-coms on TV. And practically everyone admits that we have too much personal and national debt.

Where does all this cloying, clotted superabundance come from? Obviously part of it simply derives from our wealth. We Americans are, once again, still living on the frontier in some ways; and the frontier, having struck it rich, scoffs at sumptuary laws. It likes easy credit, spending sprees, and conspicuous consumption—and so do many of us. Old money may hide discreetly behind a bourgeois façade, but not new money: in Texas and California, the nouveaux flaunt it. And we prize our eccentric millionaires, William Randolph Hearst grandly encastled in San Simeon, Howard Hughes weirdly ensconced in his Las Vegas suite, and H. Ross Perot looking to buy the White House. Why not, it's their money. In 1972, when George McGovern proposed a confiscatory tax on annual incomes over $100,000, he caught a lot of flak—from working-class types making $10,000-15,000 who wanted to enjoy their fortune when—as they naively imagined—they finally got it.

The democratic desire for (and promotional hokum about) a share in the good life is another name for the American dream, something no politician (or editorialist) can dare put down, least of all when speaking to the poor, who want to see some of that gaudy excess all around them come their way (pouring, rather than trickling, down). But the profusion (brands of cereals, makes of shirts, cookbooks and diet books) that the non-poor enjoy also stems from their mental poverty. Clueless Americans fill up the vacuum in their lives with stuff, or at least they try to.

The things that preoccupy us (what kind of giant flat-panel TV should I buy? Does Focus Factor really make you smarter? Wendy's or Micky D's?) have, if nothing else, the value that Sartre ascribes to pornography: they infallibly distract us, and so turn our thoughts away from disturbing subjects like death, guilt, the future or the past.

The classic American commentary on this situation is Thoreau's *Walden*, where in the chapter, "What I Lived For," he delivers his famous, quasi-scriptural injunction: "Simplicity, simplicity, simplicity! I say, let your affairs be as two or three, and not a hundred or a thousand; instead of a million, count half a dozen, and keep your accounts on your thumb nail. In the midst of this chopping sea of civilized life, such are the clouds and storms and quick-sands and thousand-and-one items to be allowed for that a man has to live, if he would not flounder and go to the bottom and not make his port at all, by dead reckoning, and he must be a great calculator indeed who succeeds. Simplify, simplify."

Easier said than done, of course. Who wants the sort of monkish existence Thoreau led (penniless, celibate, cut off in his mid-forties by TB? After a few days of roughing it (limiting our worldly goods to what fits into a car trunk or backpack), we're eager to get back to civilization: Thoreau may have seen it as a "chopping sea," we might more readily invoke images of hot showers and swimming pools.

But there's no doubt that on the essential point Thoreau has Americans dead to rights. We know we ought to simplify, in the same vague, nagging sense that we know we ought to cut down on cholesterol, though, like lazy cardiac cases, we may shy away from recognizing it as a life-and-death is sue. But Thoreau insists: clutter doesn't simply cause confusion and stress, it can killl. The problem isins't primarily in our crowded closets and attics and dresser drawers. It's in the arteries of our society, in the whole fabric of our world. Massive excess alienates us from nature, from one another, and from ourselves. And if it doesn't always finish off our bodies or souls, it always impoverishes our lives. In "Andrea Del Sarto," Robert Browning said that less is more; contemporary American culture shows that more is less—and less and less.

Chapter 8

The Amerigun Way of Life

Remember New Orleans!

National Rifle Association Executive Vice President Wayne LaPierre has a new rallying cry to spotlight the importance of every American's right to keep and bear arms: "Remember New Orleans." In a speech earlier this week to the New York chapter of the Sportsmen's Association for Firearms Education, LaPierre painted a compelling picture of New Orleans residents left defenseless by Hurricane Katrina—as one-third of the city's police force deserted their posts and abandoned the streets to roving bands of looters and thugs.

Here is a partial transcript of LaPierre's rousing address:

"Picture your beloved hometown, the neighborhood where you live. Hold that image in your head. Now imagine that a massive natural disaster has transformed your beloved neighborhood into a putrid soup of splinters, muck and corpses. A massive natural disaster has pounded and ground your town into an ugly gravy of dead, toxic garbage. There's no power to run a single thing that makes a sound. There's no water to bring in hydration or carry away waste. All life is stagnant around you—and dying. You can't call anyone. No one can call you. Phone lines and cell towers are down. 911 is gone. Police, fire, ambulance—the safety net of normal life—is completely gone. Think about what that would feel like. There's no one but you.

"The shadows of armed looters and thugs begin combing the streets with hard eyes and hungry looks. They take what they want. They rape who they want. They kill at will. Every exit is impassable, so leaving is impossible. But staying is unimaginable. Life has been reduced to merely breathing, devoid of the barest essentials. Your throat throbs for water. Your gut aches for food. And both hungers are eclipsed by the inevitable fight for survival against those who would take your home, your wife and your life.

"It's a hellish nightmare of hopelessness, helpless terror—bigger than your brain can almost imagine . You hear nothing but the buzz of mosquitoes, occasional shouts for help—and gunshots and looting in the dark.

"But you have a firearm.

"At dawn, a few neighbors emerge from their houses. Some of them also have guns. And you get together with them and you agree to take a stand—just as good people have done since civilization was formed. Until civilization returns, you band together to protect those who can't protect themselves. You realize suddenly that you're part of the militia in the truest historic sense of the word. You've got a lot of single mothers with kids on your street. . . . Everyone's doors and windows are wide open—they've been destroyed. So you tell the single mothers: 'If you have any trouble, just scream. We'll hear you. We'll be there.'

"You spray paint sheets of plywood with big red letters—'We are home. We have guns. We will shoot.' And you know, because even the New York Times carried a picture of it—that's exactly what they did in neighborhood after neighborhood all over the Gulf states. Not in some foreign country—here in the U.S.A. Roving gangs see your sign, they see your guns and what do they do? They stay away. Those guns and nothing else during that time gave the hopeless hope. . . . In the midst of all that misery you're struck at that moment by the beauty and the salvation of second amendment freedom in the United States of America. . . .

"The armed authorities finally arrive. They blame a broken levee for your predicament. But then, something you couldn't imagine happening, happens. They destroy the one thing that was standing there between you and anarchy—the second amendment.

"They start confiscating firearms from the law abiding. Swat-style teams start swarming block-by-block as if on a war footing. They're tense, they're jumpy and they're trained for urban warfare . Keep in mind, these military folks, these police folks—they were on our side. They didn't want to carry out this order that was given by the police chief of New Orleans.... In fact, they were outraged over what they'd been ordered to do. A reporter asked one of them—'You mean [you might have to] shoot an American?' And the soldier said 'yes.' But the

Americans he was talking about shooting, they weren't criminals. They were brave people who were simply left behind when the hurricane hit in one of the most corrupt cities in the United States of America.

"New Orleans was the first city in American history to disarm peaceable American citizens door-to-door at gunpoint. And I'll tell you this as we sit here today—it must be the last . With your help, the National Rifle Association is going to make sure it never happens again. We're going to go state-by-state and change every state law that has some type of emergency powers statute that allows authorities to regulate or confiscate guns from law abiding citizens when an emergency is declared . The example of New Orleans is going to become to worst fear of those who want to ban guns in the good old U.S.A. Never again can the anti-gunners claim that honest citizens don't need firearms because the police and the government are going to be there to protect you . And we've got a good slogan that you're going to hear from one end of the country to the other. And that slogan is: Remember New Orleans. . . .

"The next time anyone says to you: 'Are you just afraid or paranoid?' Look them straight in the eye and say: Remember New Orleans.

"If they ask you, 'Why does anyone need to own a gun?': Remember New Orleans.

"If they say to you, "Why does anyone need a high-capacity magazine?" Look them straight in the eye and say: Remember New Orleans.

"What's wrong with a 15 day waiting period? Remember New Orleans.

"What makes you think the government would ever confiscate your gun? Remember New Orleans.

"Is the second amendment relevant in the 21st Century? Remember New Orleans.

"That's our battle cry and let's never, ever let them forget it."

—www.davidduke.com/general/remember-new-Orleans_439.html
(10/31-2005)

Sorry about that elephantine quotation, (and thanks to David Duke) but to savor the absurdity (and hypocrisy and methodical mendacity) of the country's most powerful lobby, you have to let its spokesmen rant at length and warm to their theme. Not as emotionally effective, perhaps, as then-NRA President Charlton Heston's post-Mosaic defining moment in 2000 when he waved a rifle before thousands of the assembled faithful and swore that Al Gore would rip that precious symbol of his Second Amendment rights only "from my cold, dead hand"—but emphatic enough.

What's with the gun-nuts? In the wake of the April 16, 2007 Virginia Tech bloodbath you might assume that nobody needs to be reminded about the horrific toll that guns in general and handguns in particular exact every year in the US—ca. 30,000 corpses, give or take. There are—what? 250,00,000? 280,000,000? guns in private American hands. We know that no other country in the First World comes remotely close to that—or would ever tolerate it. We know about the lunacy of selling assault weapons and Saturday-night specials in stores and at gun shows and under the table to every red-blooded sociopath. But from the spectacular bloodbaths (the 1984 San Diego McDonald's massacre, the Columbine High School slaughter, the John Allen Muhammad-Lee Boyd Malvo killing spree, the Omaha mall shootings) to the ho-hum, everyday drive-by, drug-deal-gone-wrong, or love-triangle shootings, it's simply something we've gotten used to. It's that Second Amendment thing.

Which turns out, on closer inspection, to be a national psychosis, with Americans stashing those quarter-billion guns in car trunks, glove compartments, gun racks, night table drawers, etc., with 48 states allowing citizens to carry some sort of concealed weapon, with the new vogue for shooting-in-self-defense laws, and the usual ubiquitousness of guns blazing up the TV screen and the movies. Presidential candidates suddenly go hunting, join the NRA, or remember their lifelong love for plugging varmints. Whatever the Second Amendment actually means (legal scholars differ; but, given the two-centuries-plus gulf separating us and the Founders, who cares?), we could obviously tame our gun-nuts and stanch the national hemorrhage with a package of ordinary laws—if we wanted to. But we don't.

And, needless to say, there's absolutely no end in sight After the Virginia Tech massacre pundits and politicos naturally talked about—no, not gun control, heaven forfend, but the possibility of arming teachers (or students) and even—in a flight of liberal fantasy—keeping guns out of the hands of certified maniacs . Non-controversial, you say. Even the NRA, which more or less dictates what all political candidates say about guns, thinks it's a good idea, though they wouldn't go so far as to actually speak out in favor of it. But the opposition isn't so restrained. Not surprisingly, Gun Owners of America, praised by libertarian idol Ron Paul of Texas as "the only no-compromise gun lobby in Washington," strongly supports the right of mental patients' right to buy as many pieces as they need. More surprisingly, so does another rather different Washington lobby, Mental Health America, which doesn't want nosy law enforcement types or gun dealers poking into the medical records of people who have been, um, involuntarily committed to psychiatric institutions. In the face of opposition from these and other berserker-enablers, rational politicians like Congresswoman Carolyn McCarthy, who's been toiling for years to limit the bloodbath, don't stand a chance. Nor do we.

The most obvious proof of that is the nearly perfect silence on gun control that greets the daily eruptions of firearm violence across the country. We hear the usual numbing nonsense about "the signs that were missed," the warnings on the killers' web sites, the copycat syndrome, the comments by friends and neighbors of the perpetrators who are, or aren't, full of stunned surprise. But mostly we get the solemn platitudes from degreed psychobabblers about the care and feeding of the sociopaths in our midst. Then, once all the politicians, community leaders, school principals, hospital spokespersons, etc. have uttered the official national mantra about the victims' and their relatives being in our thoughts and prayers, the grief counselors can move in to soothe everyone's soul.

As one sensational episode gives way to the next, the out-to-lunch news media batten on the irresistible story-lines (Mild-mannered teen on rampage! Baby caught in crossfire! Teacher dies making herself human shield! Killer commits suicide!), even while essentially treating the shootings as spontaneous but freakish natural disasters, instead of as the predictable weather-events that they've long since become.

And not long afterwards the talking heads will chatter gaily about the pistol-packing granny who scared away a would-be intruder, or the curious surge in the number of women at firing ranges. And did you catch the burst of avuncular grins and chuckles on cable-TV programs when word got out on December 10, 2007 about the five-year old boy from Arkansas, Tre Merritt, who shot a 440-pound black bear, whose corpse was duly displayed on camera. (And—how great is this?—the kid's "10th great-grandfather" was . . . Davy Crockett!) Don'tcha love it?!

If you don't, you can always leave it—or, failing that, hope your own nearest and dearest don't go down in a hail of bullets from a weapon wielded by one of the millions of your psychopathic fellow Americans.

Chapter 9

From Barbarism to Decadence Without Passing through You-Know-What

> *Alas, for the South! Her books have grown fewer—*
> *She never was much given to literature.*

In the lamented J. Gordon Coogler, author of these elegiac lines, there was the insight of a true poet. He was the last bard of Dixie, at least in the legitimate line. Down there a poet is now almost as rare as an oboe-player, a dry-point etcher or a metaphysician. It is, indeed, amazing to contemplate so vast a vacuity. One thinks of the interstellar spaces, of the colossal reaches of the now mythical ether. Nearly the whole of Europe could be lost in that stupendous region of worn-out farms, shoddy cities and paralyzed cerebrums: one could throw in France, Germany and Italy, and still have room for the British Isles. And yet, for all its size and all its wealth and all the "progress" it babbles of, it is almost as sterile, artistically, intellectually, culturally, as the Sahara Desert. There are single acres in Europe that house more first-rate men than all the states south of the Potomac.

—H.L. Mencken, *The Sahara of the Bozart* (1917)

Sure, sure, Mencken was way over the top, even back then. And he couldn't foresee the glorious renaissance, or naissance, of southern literary greatness, from Faulkner to Allen Tate to Larry McMurtry. But was that splendid flowering actually so splendid? Isn't the American South, outside of a few lonely islands like the Research triangle and UT

Austin, still culturally sterile? And, come to think of it, even as millions of American high schoolers pore over the sacred American Scriptures of *The Red Badge of Courage, The Crucible,* and *To Kill a Mocking Bird*, as college students strain to appreciate the towering genius of *The Awakening, Howl,* and *Beloved.* and as graduate students and assistant professors from the madrasa of post-modernity plumb the funky depths of gender, desire, and foregrounded otherness in the meta-canon du jour (Adrienne Rich, Yusef Komunyakaa, Louise Erdrich, et al.), the basic question remains to be answered: how good is all this stuff?

And the basic answer is: not very. Not compared with the competition. In 1607 when the Virginia Company settlers landed on Jamestown island, Shakespeare was putting the finishing touches on *Antony and Cleopatra*. The colonists were naturally too busy to bother themselves with the theater, and it would be more than a 150 years before the first American play, Thomas Godfrey's *The Prince of Parthia* (1759) , also a romantic tragedy, but something less than immortal, appeared. As a matter of fact, for a variety of reasons including religious taboos, America never would produce an outstanding dramatist, not only no Shakespeare, but no Webster, no Molière, no Congreve, no Ibsen, no Chekhov, no Brecht, no Beckett. And by a cruel twist the two most celebrated names in American drama, Eugene O'Neill and Arthur Miller, both happened to have tin ears—it's hard to find a single resounding line or shapely sentence or memorable phrase in all their earnest *oeuvre*. Oh well, we did better with the movies.

By the second half of the 19th century America did manage to give the world two fine poets in Walt Whitman and Emily Dickinson, but they were no match for the rich European harvest of Goethe, Pushkin, Leopardi, Heine, Tennyson, Baudelaire, and so on. The novel was an even sadder business, with gifted but limited artists like Hawthorne and Melville looking altogether provincial next to Stendhal, Flaubert, George Eliot, Turgenev, Dostoyevsky and Tolstoy.

While Europe was enjoying its *anni mirabiles* in classical music, from Bach to Mozart to Beethoven to Tchaikovsky, the U.S. was preparing to unleash . . . Charles Ives? Over the century or so from *The Critique of Pure Reason* (1781) to, say, *The Genealogy of Morals* (1887)— with Hegel, J.S. Mill, Darwin, and Karl Marx in between—by which time William James had not quite finished his *Principles of Psychology* (1890), America made a few modest contributions to philosophy. The French were charmed by Benjamin Franklin and called him a *philosophe*, but that, of course, meant an amateur. Meanwhile, European geniuses like Sigmund Freud, Émile Durkheim, and Max Weber, for whom there were no American equivalents, were warming up in the bull-pen.

The literary picture improved in the 20th century (even as the generations of Old Masters faded), though there would never be an American Proust, Joyce, Kafka or even Thomas Mann. American poetry improved considerably, with Anglo-philiac T.S. Eliot taking top honors, but there would be no Yankee Yeats, Cavafy, or Lorca., not to mention Hardy, Rilke, or Valéry. The frontier ain't such a good place fer litrachoor.

This is the great unmentionable truth hovering over all the lit-crit mills of America's industrial-strength university system, hiding behind all the American Studies (and Creative Writing) programs, the arch little literary magazines, the writers colonies, the National Book awards and Pulitzer prizes, and the canonization of nonentities like Charles Steinbeck, Henry Miller, Charles Bukowski, and, yes, Ernest Hemingway: the American literary tradition is a distinctly minor league affair.

And African-American literature—let's be honest here—is largely forgettable, with nary a single first-class poet, novelist, or playwright. Musicians, yes, writers, no: Figures like Langston Hughes, Ralph Ellison, and Zora Neale Hurston had mild-but-unexceptional talents; and people who claim otherwise are thinking politically, not aesthetically. (See Chapter 20, "Culture is So Over.")

Of course, the only way to prove such slash-and-burn assertions would be through a massive series of unsparing *explications du texte*, something evidently impossible here. But for a quick-and-dirty sample, let's leave aside obvious, slow-moving targets like the ecstatically celebrated Maya Angelou and consider the stilted second paragraph of *Invisible Man*, widely hailed as a deathless masterpiece:

"Nor is my invisibility exactly a matter of a biochemical accident to my epidermis. This invisibility to which I refer"—**a typical ponderous touch** —"occurs because of a peculiar disposition of the eyes of those"—**note the three consecutive "of"s**—"with whom I come in contact. A matter of the construction of their *inner* eyes with which they look through their physical eyes upon reality."—**more dull declamation**—"I am not complaining, nor am I protesting either."—**Really?**—"It is sometimes advantageous to be unseen, although it is most often rather wearing on the nerves. Then too, you're constantly being bumped against by"—**weak use of passive voice**—"those of poor vision"—**what a feeble, amateurish phrase**—"Or again, you doubt if you really exist."—**Absurd.**—

"You wonder whether you aren't simply a phantom in other people's minds. Say, a figure in a nightmare which the sleeper tries with all his strength"—**more flat writing**—"to destroy. It's when you feel like this that, out of resentment, you begin to bump people back."—**A little bargain-basement Dostoevsky there**—"And, let me confess"—**prissy**—"you feel that way most of the time. You ache with the need to convince yourself that you do exist in the real world, that you're a part of all the sound and anguish"—**to coin a lumpy, pretentious phrase**—"and you strike out with your fists, you curse, and you swear to make them recognize you. And, alas, it's seldom successful." How's that last sentence for polite flavorlessness disguised as understatement? *This* is great writing? Nope, just another overrated American classic.

The failure of American whites, blacks, browns, reds, or yellows to win, or deserve, admission to the literary pantheon is perfectly explainable by all sorts of historical, cultural, sociological, etc. reasons; but it's nonetheless a fact. We're provincials, and always have been. We're the victims of history (isn't everybody?) Like a shabby sort of Romans, we were too busy building an empire (and slaying barbarians and managing our slaves) to have much time or respect for the arts; and now it's too late: we've missed our chance, and have become a major country with a minor culture, except maybe for jazz and other black music. (Thank God, at least, for European Jew-hatred—without it, we'd have missed those massive infusions of artistic and scientific and intellectual gold from the Haskalah.) And now, of course, with the Tower-of-Babel immigration patterns, brainy people of every description are flocking to our shores, even as we enter a globalized post-cultural era where distinct national traditions lose strength and coherence.

But, no matter, we'll cling to our feeble *Kulturgut*, an ill-favored thing, but our own. So let's celebrate our second-raters, our Washington Irvings, James Fenimore Coopers, Harriet Beecher Stowes, Henry Wadsworth Longfellows, George Whitefield Chadwicks, John Lafarges, Thomas Hart Bentons, and their numberless epigones.

As the NPR motto has it, "A great nation deserves great art." Could be, but "deserving" doesn't guarantee you anything: just turn on the TV, check the Best Sellers list, see what wins the Oscars, look at last year's Christmas, birthday, etc. cards, listen to your neighborhood church choir, or just get in your car and take an architectural tour of your usual commute to work. That should do it.

Chapter 10

Hats Off, Guys

> Remsen (Ira Remsen, d. 1927, American chemist) never wore his hat inside the door, for he had much the same respect for his laboratory that most of us have for a church.
>
> —F. H. Getman, *The Life of Ira Remsen* (1940)

When did wearing baseball caps backwards come into vogue? At some point in the '80s? When did it become all but universal? When hip-hop triumphed? At any rate the mode is now ubiquitous among young American males; and as a college teacher I've long observed, and instinctively despised, it. A few years ago, even as classrooms began filling up with backwards-capped students, I started banning *all* headgear (except yarmulkes for observant Jews and kufis for Muslims—I'm secular, but not as militantly secular as the French government), whether worn forwards, backwards, or sideways, in my classes. Some students seem taken back by this edict; and the occasional bewildered or wounded look I see in their eyes has prompted me to explain.

No doubt this is mostly a generational thing. When I was a small boy sixty years ago, my mother and grandmother taught me that one doffed one's hat inside the house. The idea, they said or implied, was to acknowledge the difference between the snowy, rainy, or torrid outdoors and the comfort of room temperature. If only as a grateful gesture to the residents, who had taken the trouble to provide a welcoming environment, one always took one's hat (and coat) off. (Paradoxically women wore their hats in church, but that was a vestige of the days when they had to be veiled.) Out in the western USA cowboys might keep their hats on in diners and bars (as dopey country music balladeers now wear their cowboy hats everywhere to proclaim their rich rural culture), but elsewhere *civilized* people removed theirs. (Hence that peculiar, servile, and now vanished institution, the hatcheck girl.)

In olden days one removed or tipped one's hat as a sign of respect or awe. In Book VI of the *Iliad* Hector "of the shining helmet" sensitively removes his trademark headpiece (it's upsetting his son); and nice guys have been doing the same ever since. The original Quaker, George Fox (d. 1691), made a dramatic, eccentric statement by noting in his journal, "When the Lord sent me forth into the world, He forbade me to put off my cap to any, high or low." Fox never guessed that three centuries later millions would follow his example, not as bold religious nonconformists, but as thoughtless devotees of secular fashion.

Well, fashion has gotten a lot more informal since then; dress codes have disappeared; even imprisoned felons now wear their beards and style their hair any way they please—which seems perfectly sensible. So, at a time when most male professors have swapped their coats and ties (not to mention academic gowns) for sweaters or sport shirts, why not let students wear baseball hats, backwards or otherwise, in the classroom?

One thing shaping my own decision was the obvious anti-intellectual symbolism of wearing the backwards cap to school: it's a way of thumbing your nose (though who does *that* anymore?) at college, of proclaiming, "Dumb And Proud Of It," or "Don't ask me," or "Hey, man, they made me come here, but they can't make me *like* it." Any doubt that these and similar Bart Simpsonesque messages are being sent by many, though not all, cap-wearers can be dispelled by the vacant, sullen, smirking, or disgusted expressions on their faces.

The baseball cap is a sort of tribal token. When I was growing up, people often wore caps, but the only ones to regularly wear them backwards were baseball catchers, who had no choice. For anyone else that would have seemed pointless—unless they were just trying to look cute—since the main purpose of baseball caps, apart from hiding a bad hair day, is to shield the eyes from the sun. Caps were seldom worn in winter (too flimsy). Farmers and other outdoor workers might wear caps to absorb sweat from their scalp or keep the dust or hay out of their hair (not a problem in the classroom). Others might wear them to symbolize their connection to a company or to advertise their allegiance to a team, a town, a school, a band, a beer, or some other product. For years fans of the New York Yankees, the Chicago Bulls, the Green Bay Packers,

John Deere tractors, etc. have been flaunting their loyalty that way, which is fine with me.

Yet nowadays the logos printed or embroidered on baseball caps are increasingly an object of indifference to the wearer. (And when worn backwards they can't directly proclaim one's support for anything.) That, it sometimes seems to me, is precisely the point. They're not worn to cheer for anything specific (being a *real* fan would be naive and uncool, better any random, meaningless name), but as a generic badge to show that one belongs to Generation X or the Young and the Bored or the Dudes with Attitude. For a while now, older, more important people, such as George Bush, Sr. or Bill Clinton or Bill Cosby, have been donning baseball caps when they want to show that they're off duty, taking a break, etc. Rich people can always wear them to pretend that they're just like everyone else, that they know how to be, or look, casual. So caps are now our lowest common sartorial denominator. But wearing them backwards goes beyond that; it tells the capless, "I'm just one of the guys.—By the way, who are you?"

Still, everyone knows that there are many occasions and places where baseball hats would be inappropriate: at weddings and bar mitzvahs, in confessionals and funeral parlors, banks and other offices, courts, sessions of Congress, TV news broadcasts, consultations with doctors, lawyers, parole boards, or executions, and so forth. Most students would, presumably, take their caps off to engage in lovemaking or eat Thanksgiving dinner. Or would they? I wonder.

By wearing them in the classroom they're making it abundantly clear that school is No Big Deal, an attitude that might well bother someone who had passionately or deliberately chosen to be a teacher. It certainly bothers me. So I demand that students remove their headgear. In fact I occasionally bark out the order in German—*Mützen ab!*—as if to admit, and savor the admission, that I know I look like a Prussian, if not a Nazi, martinet. I can't stop them from filling every gap in their conversation with "like," or noting à propos of anything unpleasant that it "sucks," or preferring Adam Sandler to Oscar Wilde or Mariah Carey to Elly Ameling or MTV to PBS or rap to rep—and so on and so forth. I can't even get them to do the reading, for God's sake. But I can, for an hour of class time, make them bare their heads, as if (but let's not kid ourselves) out of awe for the process of learning. A very minor skirmish in the cultural wars, but perhaps not a wholly idle one.

Chapter 11

The Canting of America

> And I know that I'll hear from them for this. But throwing God out successfully with the help of the federal court system, throwing God out of the public square, out of the schools. The abortionists have got to bear some burden for this because God will not be mocked. And when we destroy 40 million little innocent babies, we make God mad. I really believe that the pagans, and the abortionists, and the feminists, and the gays and the lesbians who are actively trying to make that an alternative lifestyle, the ACLU, People for the American way—all of them who have tried to secularize America—I point the finger in their face and say, "You helped this happen."
>
> —Rev. Jerry Falwell, explaining 9/11
> (quoted from John F. Harris, "'God Gave Us What We Deserve, Falwell Says'," *The Washington Post*, Sept. 14, 2001).

It's a bad sign when there's a plague raging, but people don't even know what to call it. (Remember at the dawn of the AIDS era in the early '80s when there was talk of "gay cancer"?) Thanks especially to the religious right and Republican jingoists, we have toxic levels of cant in our atmosphere, but one never hears the word itself. It was famously described by that grand old conservative, Samuel Johnson (back in the 18th century, when conservatives weren't necessarily clods or creeps or both, as they are now), speaking to Boswell: "My dear friend, clear your *mind* of cant. You may *talk* as other people do: you may say to a man, 'Sir, I am your most humble servant.' You are *not* his most humble servant. You may say, 'These are bad times; . . .' You don't mind the times. You tell a man, 'I am sorry you had such bad weather the last day of your journey, and were so much wet.' You don't care six-pence whether he is wet or dry. You may *talk* in this manner; it is a mode of talking in Society; but don't *think* foolishly" (May 2, 1783).

Once again, the unfortunate thing about this classic jolt of honesty is that most Americans wouldn't know what to make of it: the word "cant" itself has now fallen out of usage, and no synonym or quick definition can do justice to its richness. To quote only one section of the *Oxford English Dictionary's* entry for the verb "to cant" : "6. . . . To affect religious or pietistic phraseology, *esp.* as a matter of fashion or profession; to talk unreally or hypocritically with an affectation of goodness or piety."

A moment's reflection will reveal that this country is awash in cant. Consider some of the phony-pious locutions that have crept into our language recently: "the war on terror" (between Goodness Incarnate [us] and Evil Incarnate [them], fought by "smart bombs," torture, and trashing the Constitution), "God bless America" (=Hey, we're the Umpire's kids; He's *gotta* call the game our way), "Our thoughts and prayers are with you" (=Oops, sorry about that—whatever), I support "the culture of life" (=unlike those filthy baby-killers), "I believe in traditional marriage" (=I'm a pillar of freely chosen heterosexual rectitude, unlike those swinish "liberals"), "Free Market Economy" (=any system rigged in favor of Dick Cheney and his friends"), "Support our troops" (that little yellow-ribbon decal on the back of my car makes all the difference in the world), etc.

Then there are the quick-and-dirty code-words: "democracy" (=practically flawless, uniquely American brand of political wisdom, offered gratis to incompetent, ungrateful Third World countries), "patriotism" (=screaming-eagle, my-flag-pin's-bigger-than-yours chauvinism), "heroes" (=any Americans who happen to die—or survive—while wearing a uniform), "al Qaeda" (=any Muslim fighters we haven't caught or killed yet/ any evil force we can't quite locate), "family values" (=conservative, Christian sexual standards, exclusively obtainable from sanctimonious Republican mantra-chanters, regardless of their personal behavior or earlier positions), "class-warfare" (= any attempt, or favorable mention of an attempt, to squeeze a little more tax money out of the rich),. or "socialized medicine" (=health care for the lower classes).

Naked lies and vicious half-truths aside, there's nothing necessarily wrong with political rhetoric, so long as its consumers realize it's rhetoric.

Americans, however, often naively take it at face value. They imagine—some of them, anyhow—that this really is "the land of the free and the home of the brave" (what about those 2.1 million people in prison?), that there really is "liberty and justice for all" (an utter impossibility—would you accept "for 71% of the population"?), that the USA really is, *tout court*, the "greatest country in the world" (measured by what—the defense budget? per capita energy-extravagance? the number of products for sale in suburban New Jersey?) We can say, or sing, such lines, but we needn't swallow the cant they proclaim. (We're proud to proclaim ourselves "one nation, under God"; but, if there were a God, wouldn't all nations, like it or not, have to be "under" him? Or is it that we chosen ones bow beneath Yahweh's scepter in our own uniquely wonderful way?)

Cant so predominates in the public forum that, like bad money, it drives out solid, honest opinion. The list of things one mustn't say stretches out to the horizon. TV newsfolk sing hosannas to IV-F-concocted multiple births and picturesquely large-to-huge families, whereas the breeders involved have only made the world more crowded, not to mention the colossal expense and medical problems created by anomaly-ridden preemies. But you don't dare say that, or, still less, that one solution to the overwhelming burden of patients far gone with Alzheimer's and other varieties of dementia might be to do to them what we do to our dogs and cats when they're too far gone. Nor can local TV reporters fail to greet every recreational drug bust with understated smug approval. Somehow a little less pot our there makes us all a little safer—or something.

And then there's patriotism, unforgettably defined by Dr. Johnson as "the last refuge of a scoundrel" (See Chapter 3, "Scoundrels in the Last Refuge"). We already have way too much flag-waving as it is. (In the innocent days long before 9/11 an otherwise red-blooded American, Joe Namath, proposed that we skip playing "The Star Spangled Banner" before *every* game, but he was indignantly hooted down.) And since 9/11, well, we've been buried in a blizzard of patriotic color. Personally, I've been so angered by the proliferation of mini-flags and flag-stickers, along with "Support the Troops" magnets, on cars belonging to the sunshine patriots in my town (Schenectady, NY) that whenever I see one parked with no driver in sight, I leave the following flyer attached to the windshield—then I hightail it out of there.

Dear American Flag-Waver:

All of us are thrilled to see your patriotic display. Nevertheless, like all great symbols, Old Glory can be understood in many ways. So, would it be possible for you to post a sign explaining exactly what this showing of the red, white and blue means:

1. *Do you support President Bush's invasion of Iraq based on deliberate lies about non-existent WMDs?*
2. *Do you support the slaughter of 150,000+ Iraqi civilians, many of them killed by Americans?*
3. *Do you support the Iraqi civil war that our invasion has caused (4 million refugees so far)?*
4. *Do you support the spread of terrorism in Iraq and worldwide that four years of war have launched?*
5. *Do you support the sacrifice of over 4,000 American lives (+ 30,000 wounded) for nothing?*
6. *Do you support the Shiite fanatics now brutally oppressing Iraqi women with help from the US?*
7. *Do you support spending a trillion dollars on a horrific war led by a deranged, incompetent draft-dodger?*

Needless to say, it's a losing battle (which is why I don't wait around to engage in dialogue with the patriotic jerk-motorist) : I'm hopelessly outnumbered by the flag waving America-firsters, many of whom would doubtless love to rattle their sabers as well, if only they had one. It's the old myth: individually we may be fallible and even (at times) mistaken, even as collectively we're divine. But the nation's mind is as clotted with cant as its arteries are with fat. Is there a Doctor Johnson in the house?

Chapter 12

It's Offal, It's Awful, It's All We've Got

> Through want of enterprise and faith, men are what they are, buying and selling, and spending their lives like serfs.
>
> —Thoreau, *Walden*, "Baker Farm"

If the center of domestic life in America is the kitchen (with the TV room right next to it—unless, as often happens, the kitchen too has a TV set), then the center of public life has to be the mall, with the ganglia of roads leading to and from the metastasized shopping center. And, ditzy shopoholics aside, the depression sets in before you even get out of your car: just one look at those oceanic (or is it desert-like?) parking lots, whether crammed or empty, the perfect symbol of sterile, mindless functionality, stretching out, if not exactly *à perte de vue*, then more than far enough. Don't forget the sector you're parked in—wait, was it E4? C4?—or you may never get to go home.

Forget the market-place, the town square, the biblical "gates of the city." Welcome to Consumerlandia, where every dose is an overdose. It's something like the nursing home syndrome: take an aging, decrepit, perhaps demented human being. This is a normal and, barring euthanasia, unavoidable sight (memento mori, we'll all get there eventually, etc.) But multiply the one sad instance by a couple of dozen or a couple of hundred and stow all the urine-scented specimens under one roof; and even observers resigned to their own mortality may find it hard to bear. Ditto for the more-is-less profusion of stores in the mall: Aeropostale,

Arby's, Bally Total Fitness, Banana Republic, Barnes & Noble, Bath and Body Works, Brookstone, Candy Express, Circuit City, CVS, Dairy Queen, Dick's Sporting Goods, Dollar Store, Express, Famous Footware, Foot Locker, Frederick's of Hollywood, GAP, Guess, Harry & David, Home Depot, J. C. Penney, Kaybee Toys, Limited, Macy's Nail Art, Nextel, Old Navy, Payless Shoe Store, Pottery Barn, Radio Shack, Ruby Tuesday, S & K Menswear, Subway, Sunglass Hut, The Body Shop, Vitamin World, Walmart , Williams Sonoma, Yankee Candle Co., Zales—and that barely scratches the surface. To crown this movable feast (stores opening or closing every month) there's the mall cineplex, now almost the only place you can see movies. These days the menu may be large, with eight to twelve or more theaters, but almost all of them are bound to be showing dreadful stuff like *Rush Hour 3*, *Norbit*, *Evan Almighty*, or *I Am Legend*, all with fifteen minutes or so of trailers for equally dreadful future offerings. Now please turn off your cell phone and enjoy the show!

Unlike the classical market place, malls are the scene of precious little socializing, gossiping, or meeting friends and neighbors (except the ones you trucked in with you). There's no chit-chat between the salespeople (most of whom would clearly rather be somewhere else) and the customers. There are no windows, no climate, no air. The atmosphere has been neutralized down to nothing, other than those yummy fried fat odors wafting from the food court. The whole thing has no center, no graspable shape, no rhythm—except that of the joylessly grinding mills of the Free Market Economy. Consumers *must* keep coming back for more and more and more, buying all kinds of stuff they don't really need with money they don't really have, or the FME will go into recession or worse. Only 287 shopping days till Christmas, so get out there and do your part. *Citius, altius, fortius.*

But let's not forget some useful non-purchasing services provided by malls: a politics-free zone, where all forms of electioneering, picketing, protesting, leafletting, and controversial-issue-raising are forbidden (as conversation is in church), a rendez-vous point for idle teens, a promenade-track for cardiological athletes, and, of course, a treasure trove for shoplifters (plus some limited opportunities for parking-lot muggers and deranged shooters in Goth get-up).

Still more importantly, malls serve to distract the entire citizenry from their tedious, empty lives. There is, notoriously, a lack of meaningful public space (such as the parks of central London or the boulevards of Paris, or the piazzas and cafes all over Italy) in American cities;

and though not esthetically pleasing or otherwise inviting, the malls *are* public; so whenever Keats's "melancholy fit"—or that November-in-the-soul feeling described by Melville—descends, when there's nothing on TV, and you're bored out of your mind, you know where you can go, as long as you've got wheels or can stand the bus. Imagine how great a venue it would have been for the Ancient Mariner, with all those buttonholeable passers-by. Not so good, however, for the rest of us.

Still more crucially, imagine the malls being flung open to mobs of Third-Worlders with shopping carts (and donated cash) to haul away things they have a pressing need for, as opposed to all the listless Americans wandering amid the racks and stacks and cabinets and cases, vitrines and wall-mounted displays of items they likely have already. Poverty-stricken pilgrims to Cornucopia Capitalistica would presumably be more impressed by its lavishness than by its wastefulness or numbing reduplication: countless brands, the bulk of them little better or worse than the others, of everything, jeans, sneakers, mascara, eyeglass frames, cell phones, parkas, stuffed toys, Chia pets, diapers (baby and adult), costume jewelry, hex wrenches, chocolates, MP3 players, luggage, CDs, air conditioners, lingerie, watches, sports jerseys, perfume, spark plugs, steak knives, shampoo, brushes, laptops . . . you know, everything.

Faced with all this, the shoppers look overmatched: mostly bored and disconnected, they plod down the aisles in search of whatever, or else drift along empty-handed, barely registering the sights of the Cyclopean smorgasbord around them. As if the sheer volume of the offerings wasn't enough, they come packaged in prodigious amounts of cardboard, cellophane, bubble wrap, and plastic of every description—all destined, of course, for the mountainous pile of the next garbage-collection.

Sometimes, in fact, the life-cycle of American consumer goods seems to go from trash to trash, as surely as that of their purchaser is from ashes to ashes and from dust to dust. As Heather Rogers points out in her illuminating *The Hidden Life of Garbage* (2005), 80% of all US products are used only once and then discarded. And everyone knows we lead the world in the spectacular, shameless volume of it all: something on the order of a quarter-billion tons of garbage produced every year, the vast majority of it never to be recycled, with the average citizen contributing over a ton and half to the pile, six times more per capita than the rest of the world. But where would we American serfs be without it?

Chapter 13

Sludge, Slime, and Saccharine

> We have so many people who can't see a fat man standing beside a thin one without coming to the conclusion that the fat man got that way by taking advantage of the thin one. So they are going to solve all the problems of human misery through government and government planning. . . . We were told four years ago that 17 million people went to bed hungry each night. Well, that was probably true. They were all on a diet.
>
> —Ronald Reagan, TV speech, September 27, 1964

Anyone old enough to remember what a horrible president Ronald Reagan was had to keep pinching himself or herself during Ronnie's bloated, mendacious exequies. For the better part of a week (June 5-11, 2004, ending on a national day of mourning), it seemed as if the entire country had succumbed to tender-minded amnesia, with media heavies—TV reporters, anchor persons, and the commentariat in general—intoning one lyrical, soft-focus tribute after another to that wretched ex-inhabitant of the White House.

But, then again, this gooey dissolve into clichés about The Great Communicator was only fitting; because of all the elements that made for Ronald Reagan's remarkable success, one of the most important was the way he satisfied, or pandered to, America's appetite for sentimentality. Consider the patented Reagan delivery: the shy, self-effacing, just-folksy intonation, the winks, the grins, the shrugs, the professional twinkle in the eye, the flirting with the camera, the little hitch in the voice before zinging the one-liners, the cajolery that seemed to say, "Hey, am I a regular guy *or what*? Would I talk over your head? I mean, I may be old-fashioned, but . . ."

Reagan was forever serving up platitudes or non-sequiturs or lies about balancing the budget (he was a spendthrift) or trees causing pollution (he was an ignoramus) or the reawakened militaristic "pride in America" (he was a snappy-saluting draft-dodger), but millions of otherwise sensible Americans eagerly swallowed it, because they liked his "style"—his seemingly warm and spontaneous approach (though he was in person affably aloof from almost everyone, including himself) to patriotism, religion (though he had little of it), his adoring Nancy, and the good old days of show biz (he was a crummy actor).

The American Heritage Dictionary, like most others, defines sentimental as "affectedly or extravagantly emotional," but there's more to it than that. The sentimentalist doesn't simply have emotions, he wallows in them. Sentimentalists are narcissists who have to catch their own performance. Though we talk about "sloppy sentimentality," the true sentimentalist is calculating. He shrewdly studies what his audience wants and shamelessly gives it to them. Ronald Reagan, like many others of his kind, was no fool. Knowing that the corny appeal to "win one for the Gipper" (a teary quotation from the dying George Gipp speaking of himself, in the third person, to Knut Rockne) moved his listeners, at least the ones on his team, so much that he repeated it until it became one of the all time self-referential mantras.

Sentimentality hangs as thickly over American popular culture as fog over the Grand Banks. TV, movies, bestsellers, and public discourse are drenched in it. Some obvious examples: tributes to our "fighting men and women," everything that happens on St. Patrick's Day, most Hollywood "classics": *Going My Way, Easy Rider, Dirty Dancing, Dances With Wolves, Forrest Gump*, all "family" shows (in fact, at times, the very word "family"), Christmas specials, Hallmark cards, "Peanuts" artifacts, Thomas Kinkade's paintings, etc.

The catalog could evidently be extended *ad infinitum*. The question is, why are we so susceptible to this nauseating stuff? (Many Americans think being "sentimental" is actually a very good thing, equating it with sensitivity and tenderness—even as *those* terms are off limits to red-blooded males.) Some of the blame has to go to America's shallow cultural roots: our Puritan ancestors taught us to be suspicious of art (sensual pleasure). So it wasn't until the 20th century that the country produced any drama (a little anyway) worth watching. We have little time for

Puritanism nowadays; but when it comes to the arts, for many people almost any kind of schlock will do—like once-poor immigrants buying furniture.

Our lack of standards, traditions, academies, and so forth has often proved liberating, but it's also the reason why much of the public takes middling writers like Hemingway and Steinbeck (both Nobel-Prize-winning sentimental emoters) for towering geniuses, and why for years Americans mistook Liberace (before he became a drag queen) for a great concert pianist. Democracy inculcates many virtues, but good taste isn't one of them.

Yet on the other hand, to return to Reagan, who really cares if his shtick was sloppy or maudlin, so long as it worked—which it undoubtedly, and unfortunately, did? How many people were bothered that George H. W. Bush, though unable to project Reagan's aw-shucks sincerity, readily embraced his sentimental cant ("a thousand points of light," "adoption, not abortion," etc.), as son Dubya briefly did with "compassionate conservatism"? "Just politics," we mutter; and of course there's truth in that, but there's also a nagging problem.

Political slush may seem harmless, but, like all forms of sentimentality, it's a lie and ultimately bad for the soul. We can't expect politicians to tell the truth all the time (one had to cough and look the other way when Jimmy Carter, in his anti-Nixonian zeal, swore, "I'll never lie to you"); but neither should we have passively endured the spectacle of selfishness (Reaganomics) simpering and posing as brotherly love ("a kinder, gentler America"). In the end Bush senior just wasn't a good enough actor to parlay that lame routine into a second term.

In any event, we can see pretty clearly that Reagan's eight years as president amounted to a Raw Deal for many people (e.g., the poor, AIDS patients) and causes (the environment, among others) in this country; but that even while tepid about his policies, the voters fatuously endorsed his "charm." No wonder they seldom became indignant at the "sleaze factor," at Iran-Contra, the deficit, the plight of the homeless, the kneeling to honor the SS fallen at Bitburg, the idiotic drug laws, and so forth: why launch a malpractice suit against Dr. Feelgood, when you hired him to cheer you up, not to cure what ailed you? Fair enough, but like all bad art, like all sloppy, sentimental shows viewed by an unsuckered audience, the Reagan administration, in the long run, can only produce disgust.

Writing about Reagan's death in *TomPaine.com* on June 6, 2004, David Corn wrote: "I have a vision. On the day that Ronald Ronald Reagan's remains are transported from the U.S. Capitol to the National Cathedral for the funeral services, the hearse will pass 800 black crosses. Each cross will represent one of the men, women and children who were killed by the Salvadoran military in the village of El Mozote in December 1981. Each would be a reminder that the dead man now celebrated in the media as a lover of freedom and democracy oversaw a foreign policy that empowered and enabled murderous brutes and thugs in the name of anti-Sovietism."

Interesting vision, but fat chance. Years earlier, in *The Nation* on March 2, 1998, Corn had provided a handy list of "Sixty-Six Things to Think About When Flying in to Reagan National Airport": "The firing of the air traffic controllers, winnable nuclear war, trees that cause pollution, Elliott Abrams lying to Congress, ketchup as a vegetable, public housing cutbacks, getting cozy with Argentine fascist generals, tax credits for segregated schools, disinformation campaigns, 'homeless by choice,' Manuel Noriega, falling wages, "constructive engagement" with apartheid South Africa, the invasion of Grenada, assassination manuals, drug tests, the S&L scandal, silence on AIDS, food-stamp reductions, $640 Pentagon toilet seats, William Casey, Iran/contra, Robert Bork, naps, Ed Meese ('You don't have many suspects who are innocent of a crime'), massacres in El Salvador)"—but why go on? The lesson was pluperfectly clear, but the great majority of the students missed it.

We have, after all, applied the same sentimental glossing over to our slave-holding Founding Fathers, most notably Washington and Jefferson, to the Indian-killers who "won the West" (having previously "won the East"), to any number of "gallant" Confederate generals, Stonewall Jackson, *(such* a devout Christian, bless him), Nathan Bedford Forrest (where would the Klan be without him?), Jeb Stuart (played by Errol Flynn in *The Santa Fe Trail*), and, of course, the most lovable of all the great warriors, Robert E. Lee (master of the sorriest slaughter in American history). Then there was the recklessly insubordinate Gen. Douglas MacArthur, whose weepy send-off line about old soldiers never dying, but just fading away was immediately turned into a pop tune and vaulted him into the American pantheon. Even Richard Nixon's life of infamy has, ever since his forced resignation and gushy funeral, been sugar-coated and perfumed. Hey, didn't he sign the Endangered Species act?

There are, it seems, no limits or bottom to the slush fund of evil political sentimentality. Consider the following ditty (by Julian Wilson and James M. Smith), designed as an updated *Battle Hymn of the Republic* (itself a self-indulgent exercise in religiously tinged patriotism) to honor that emblematic Nixon-era Vietnam warrior, Lieut. William Calley, and played by radio stations across the land in 1971. (The words "My Lai," "court martial," or "guilty" are, of course, never mentioned.)

(Spoken introduction):
Once upon a time there was a little boy who wanted to grow up and be a soldier and serve his country in whatever way he could. He would parade around the house with a sauce pan on his head for a helmet, a wooden sword in one hand and the American flag in the other. As he grew up, he put away the things of a child but he never let go of the flag . . .

My name is William Calley, I'm a soldier of this land
I've tried to do my duty and to gain the upper hand
But they've made me out a villain they have stamped me with a brand
As we go marching on

I'm just another soldier from the shores of U.S.A.
Forgotten on a battle field then thousand miles away
While life goes on as usual from New York to Santa Fe
As we go marching on

I've seen my buddies ambushed on the left and on the right
And their youthful bodies riddled by the bullets of the night
Where all the rules are broken and the only law is might
As we go marching on

While we're fighting in the jungles they were marching in the street
While we're dying in the rice fields they were helping our defeat
While we're facing V.C. bullets they were sounding a retreat
As we go marching on

With our sweat we took the bunkers, with our tears we took the plain
With our blood we took the mountains and they gave it back again
Still all of us are soldiers, we're too busy to complain
As we go marching on

When I reach my final campground in that land beyond the sun
And the great commander asks me, "Did you fight or did you run?"
I'll stand both straight and tall stripped of medals, rank and gun
And this is what I'll say:

Sir, I followed all my orders and I did the best I could
It's hard to judge the enemy and hard to tell the good
Yet there's not a man among us would not have understood

We took the jungle village exactly like they said
We responded to their rifle fire with everything we had
And when the smoke had cleared away a hundred souls lay dead

Sir, the soldier that's alive is the only once can fight
There's no other way to wage a war when the only one in sight
That you're sure is not a VC is your buddy on your right

When all the wars are over and the battle's finally won
Count me only as a soldier who never left his gun
With the right to serve my country as the only prize I've won
As we go marching on
Glory, glory hallelujah

Pause for choked-up listeners to blow their noses and clear their throats: it doesn't get much better than THAT: a rabble-rousing cocktail of one part patriotic sludge, one part xenophobic slime, and one part carcinogenic saccharine. But practically no one bothered to protest against it, except the certifiably insane Hunter Thompson, who would surely be the first to remind us that you are what you drink.

Chapter 14

What We're Really Good At

> After amassing a large personal fortune, Lawrence founded the Lawrence Welk resort village. The Welk resort [near Escondido, California] is a vast complex which includes vacation time shares, gift shops, restaurants, an auditorium, the museum, and, of course, several golf courses. Lawrence was an avid golfer. Having built a lavish resort covering many square miles, Lawrence could well afford to put his personal residence within walking distance of the first tee, allowing him to golf every day. With essentially unlimited funds, what housing did Lawrence create? Lawrence created a trailer park on the resort grounds so he could place his personal triple-wide trailer next to the first tee. Lawrence Welk was consistent in his approach to both housing and music, both being the finest in mediocrity.
>
> —www.jeffreysward.com/tributes/lrm.htm

Ah, the trifecta: a perfectly dreadful but wildly popular and fabulously rich musician emerges from his de luxe trailer to disport himself, like Adam in Paradise, on the greensward of his own private Utopia. It doesn't get much more mediocre than this. And America IS the land of mediocrity. Like it or not, we've taken mediocrity to our bosom and hugged it tight. We have a mediocre (on very good days) government, mediocre (or worse) schools and colleges, a mediocre health care system (A for the best covered, F for the worst-covered-uncovered averages out to a C), and so on down the line: from our mass-produced roadside stores with their giant parking lots and their mediocre products to the multiplexes with their awful movies, from the highways clogged with SUVs to the supermarket aisles clogged with shopping carts full of fattening glop, from its proliferating fast food joints (Happy Meals!) to its proliferating mega-churches (Happy Talk!) , from its eyesore architecture (the soulless Strip) to its brainsore politics (candidate beauty contests judged by electorate-auscultating media stylists): American Dumbs-Down, Inc.—No job too large or too small.

Like jarring contrasts? There's no need to go further than America's all-purpose pharmacies, where in one convenient trip one can pick up both a drug to cure you (Lipitor, maybe) and a drug to kill you (cigs), where you can buy useful stuff for the house (toothpaste, detergents, batteries) and worthless stuff for your head (row upon row of for-idiots-only paperbacks, glossy magazines, greeting cards, "novelties," and seasonal clutter).

Talk about an embarrassment of poverties, of monetary feast and mental famine, simultaneous, supersized excess and deficit—all adding up, once more, to mediocrity. The mind, as they say, boggles. Who could take it all in? Walt Whitman himself would be left stuttering. So why not focus on one uniquely American cultural creation that combines prodigious effort, expense, planning, and ingenuity to create mostly idle amusement : Division I (and its Division I-AA, Division II and III imitators) college sports. From the playing fields of Eton to the Alabama Crimson Tide's Denny-Briant Stadium (92,000+ capacity) and its $4 million-a-year football coach, Lou Saban there may be a logical line of progression, but it's a twisted one.

As everyone knows, but nobody—except a few killjoy critics—minds, college sports are big business. Tens of millions get spent on athletic programs (the vast majority of which don't show a profit) in hopes of alumni giving, name recognition (get into the box score with the Big Guys), TV revenue, and various other access ramps to p.r. paradise. Coaches (who are technically teachers) get astronomical salaries, athletes live in a cushy welfare state (of course, some are black and poor, and can use the money), recruiting goes from intense to hysterical (aided and abetted by the helpful folks in Admissions), with the whole thing serving as a feeder to the NFL, the NBA, the NHL, and MLB, though in fact only the tiniest minority ever make it that far. "This young man," intones the awed announcer at college football games, "is going to be playing on *Sundays.*"

But it's a gorgeous spectacle: the giant stadia, field houses, and rinks jammed with screaming fans (most of them paying customers), the marching bands, the pep rallies, the butt-twitching cheerleaders, the tailgate barbecues and beer parties, the Bowl Games (32 and counting), March Madness, hovering blimps, the Rose-Orange-Cotton-Citrus-Fiesta-etc. Bowls and their Parades—all of what not-otherwise-gushy broadcasters like to call "Tradition" (with a tiny hitch in the throat, as when names of the living or dead Great Ones like Bear Bryant, Woody Hayes, Joe Paterno, John Wooden, Dean Smith, Jim Valvano, Al McGuire, etc. are mentioned). Isn't that what College is all about? The New Year's Eve we did the town, the day we tore the goal-posts down. . . .

Of course, most of the college powerhouses are located in the statistically dumbest and most backward part of the nation, the South. And a fair number of these are institutions better known for their sports mascots than for their distinguished faculty or brilliant students: the Clemson Tigers (get off exit 19B on I-85 and just follow the huge orange paw marks), the Arkansas razorbacks (woooo-pig soo-ee!), the Kentucky wildcats, the Florida gators, N.C. State wolf pack, the LSU Tigers (and the Auburn Tigers and the Mizzou Tigers: well, there are only so many cool-cum-ferocious animals to go around), and so on. Where else but in the South—where, as William Faulkner famously said, the past isn't even past—would you find the magnificent obsession of the Ole Miss campus with its 18 mile per hour speed limit, in honor of Archie Manning's jersey number? THAT is tradition, mah frens!

But college sports frenzy is obviously not limited to dumb red states, it's a national madness (though, come to think of it, New York City doesn't have a single outstanding team in any major college sport). Everyone's caught it. Quinnipiac University in Hamden, Connecticut, for example, best known for its polling institute, has just built a 52-million-dollar Banknorth Sports Center to spotlight its successful hockey squad and its maybe-burgeoning Division I basketball team.

Over thirty years ago as a teaching assistant at Harvard I had a student—let's call him Mr. Blefuscu—whose papers and exams showed an off-the-charts incompetence. How odd, I thought. Later that fall semester I happened to be at a football game in Harvard Stadium that went down to the wire. Then in the waning moments of the fourth quarter, a golden field goal opportunity loomed, and I heard the loudspeaker crackle: "Now kicking for Harvard . . . Blefuscu!" Mystery solved. And since then the Ivy League has only gotten more intoxicated with sport, though less pre-professionally so than the teams in the Top Twenty-Five.

This too is Tradition. In 1923 just before the annual Harvard-Yale game ("The Game") Yale coach T.A.D. Jones told his players, "Gentlemen, you are now going out to play football against Harvard. Never again in your whole life will you do anything so important." And I'll bet that was true for at least a few of the duller bulbs on both teams.

Now do you think we could we could sell football as a mega-sport to British and continental universities? I mean, all that hitting the books and no March Madness (Sweet Sixteen-Elite Eight-Final Four: now THAT's poetry!), no Heisman Trophy, no BCS Bowl, no College World Series, no Frozen Four, no lacrosse, track, swimming, volleyball, soccer, golf, or gymnastics teams—what a downer. Well, at least they have rowing.

Chapter 15

"News" You Can "Use"

Here comes the bride—and the groom!

A Detroit couple is among four couples vying to be married on NBC's "Today Throws a Martha Stewart Wedding": Nicole Dent and Tommy Duncan, both 27, were introduced on the show this morning and will be mentioned on the upcoming segments through Aug. 20 through the 8 a.m. hour. Each of the couples had 30 minutes to do a presentation after they were introduced on the show. The Detroit couple, dressed stylishly in black, did a ballroom dance routine to R. Kelly's "Step in the Name of Love." . . . Viewers will have till 5 p.m. Monday to vote for their favorite couple. Viewers vote by logging onto www.TodayShow.com or text messaging their votes to 4683 (with the couple's number—either 1, 2, 3, or 4). The Detroit couple is Couple No. 2. The winning couple will be married live on the show Oct. 5, making them the eighth couple to tie the know on the show. After the couple is chosen, viewers will plan their wedding by voting for her wedding dress, the attendants' attire, their rings, the flowers, the cake, the honeymoon and more from selections chosen by Martha Stewart and "Today" producers.

—Cassandra Spratling, in the *Detroit Free Press*, Aug. 15, 2007

It's amazing what passes for news these days. Even as actual newspapers fade from view in America, the drivel called TV journalism reaches new depths of insignificance. Despite the implosions of the Johnson, Nixon, and George W. Bush presidencies, the media have continued to treat the White House with near-mystical veneration, blandly echoing blatant agitprop by Bushie principals or spokespersons (from Rumsfeld to Rove to Snow to Perino), and never directly refuting (at most adding "Some critics complain that . . .") the palpable or poisonous nonsense contained in their utterances, the way reporters for, say, the BBC routinely do. (Only after the compassionate conservatives were caught committing acts of enormous, but "non-political," incompetence during and after Katrina, did the talking heads from the major networks—except, of course, for the beyond-buffoonery Fox News cheering section—belatedly start to hold them to a diluted sort of accountability.)

The idea that all reportage on the holders of staggering amounts of power—whether located in the Kremlin, Wall Street, the Vatican, or the West Wing—should be adversarial and instinctively suspicious seems not to have dawned on the regular news gang. Thus, moderately critical voices like Tim Russert and Chris Matthews now qualify as tigerish tribunes of the people.

Well, given the ideological vacuity and general puerility of the American public, it's not surprising that the news media should take a timid/sycophantic approach to politics. And, given the Nielsen-driven nature of everything on TV, it's equally unsurprising that all the subjects covered on the "news" should have the nutritional value of Cheese Puffs—at best. Thus, we get the hysterically overblown coverage of hurricanes, tornadoes, blizzards, avalanches, mudslides, ice storms, and bad weather of every description, even if it's happening thousands of miles of way from the station carrying it. The one thing we can ALL understand is weather—its effects anyhow, not the damned technical stuff like isobars and occluded fronts. In the same vein, we get stories about victims of shark and other animal attacks (never mind the billions of animals *we're* attacking and killing), about lottery winners, heroic pets, troubled celebrities (high Schadenfreude-quotient there), babies stolen from hospitals, hale-and-hearty centenarians, and survivors of *anything*, from cancer to earthquakes to hostage-situations. Best of all, apart from major catastrophes, we have those-ever-so-handy Health-Care Headlines: medical updates on obesity, Alzheimer's, mammograms, prostate cancer, FDA recalls, and the twists and turns of America's perverted health insurance industry—not just news, but potentially **life-saving information** for the minimally informed viewer.

We like our stories *personal*, so the networks spent an entire day perseverating over John Kennedy, Jr.'s missing plane in 1999—never mind that everyone knew it was beneath the waves (ditto for the dead

Crandall Canyon miners in August, 2007: the networks let company president, Bob Murray, do his obscene, grossly self-serving "It's-not-our-fault-but-oh-we-care-so-much!" marathon dance, even as the miners' bodies rotted away)—and week after week on the saga of Anna Nicole Smith. "News" about First Ladies always rates a benign smile, even as the Ladies themselves are always more popular than their mates, except for Hillary, who kept butting her nose into politics. We like our stories *simple*, so the Whitewater scandal never went anywhere; and from the invasion of Iraq until the buttons-popping moment of Mission Accomplished, the Fox News logo for all reports from Iraq showed two US soldiers with M-16s against the background of—what else?—the Twin Towers in flames. We like our stories *sexy*, so we never heard the end of Bill Clinton's erratic-erotic adventures, from Gennifer Flowers to the Great Fellatio Impeachment.

We like to have our TV "news" further personalized by being read off the teleprompter by a trusted "anchor." The fact that on any given night the three anchors are reading off more or less the same stories in more or less the same order *can* be distressing; so occasionally one fearless newshound-in-chief or another will sally forth into the real world and report to us from a war zone, G-8 summit, or Dramatic Point of Interest, perhaps dressed in combat fatigues, flak jacket, or even a guayabera.

No anchor could possibly be an expert—or have anything useful to say—on all the issues covered (however superficially in 30- or 50-second blips by the lesser reporters); but an iron rule dictates that the anchor sets up the story with an opening sentence or two and then asks the on-the-spot guy/gal a phony question, e.g., "I gather, Bill, that the President is facing some opposition on this from his own party." To which the inevitable refrain is: "Absolutely, Dan. Just today, in fact, . . ." Like pint-size, peppery Wolf Blitzer in his hyperkinetic Situation Room (forever reminding insufficiently enthusiastic viewers that CNN has "the best political team in the business"), the Anchor is nearly omniscient—whatever's lacking to his total mastery of events will be filled in by his indefatigable team of assistants. One longs in vain for the messy vagaries of real conversation, where an interlocutor might snap back, "Where'd you get *that* idea, Joe?" or "No way, that's ancient history."

But it can't happen, because entertainers have to be in perfect sync. The anchor is the m.c., guiding the performers through their paces. The usual show-biz standards apply to the reporters: women (save for an

Andrea Mitchell here and there) have to be young and dishy, men can get by with "character." And the "news," in the end, is entertainment. That's why is has to be about *us* (Waco, not Waziristan), stuff we can *relate to* (serial killers, not statistics on AIDS), *practical* info (product recalls, not problems with the ozone layer), and, above all, lots of *people-stories* (Senior citizen decks mugger! Walk-on crowned MVP! Parrot answers phone!). Keep it short and simple, i.e. dumb.

The dumbest edition of the news comes in the morning shows. Coverage gets a little, but not much, less cheesy on the cable news programs (cf. the insufferably merry *Robin and Company*, etc.), and makes a stab at high seriousness with the half-hour (24-minutes) evening news, though even then the stories covered will be Americo-centrally parochial (snowstorm in the Plains headed east vs. the climate change conference in Bali), pre-chewed for easy digesting, absurdly brief, and culminating whenever possible in some inspirational moment (woman donates kidney to stranger, couple celebrate 80th wedding anniversary, Marine dad, just back from Iraq, surprises his kids at school), as if a) to acknowledge that in these dark times we all need a little uplift, and b) to defuse any complaints that all the networks ever report is bad news. So *there*! And did we mention that Toys for Tots has never had such a great year?!

But it's *The Today Show* and its ilk that set the dismal standard and offer the most revolting example of "news" you can "use": an absurd amalgam of mini-video-bulletins with gossip (DUI starlets), idle chatter (weekend box office receipts—not, perish the thought, critical reviews—of worthless movies), recipes, diets, fashion tips, personal finance, parenting help, a bit of live music, and ludicrous in-studio spectaculars like NBC's "Martha Stewart Weddings."

Borrowing the dynamite technique of total audience involvement from reality TV, "Martha Stewart Weddings" exchanges boring passivity for populist news-*making*. Americans may not know much, but they know what they like. Besides, as occasional media-glimpses into the real world keep showing, it's a depressing scene out there. So why not create a pleasant phantasm (desert island, picturesque jungle, talent contest) where "we" call the shots. And live happily ever after in a drug-induced coma.

Chapter 16

Feelthy Peektures of All-American Guys and Gals

> RAUNCHY, SWEATY, AND DOWNRIGHT FILTHY! Amy and her amazing tits start off this extravaganza of pure, raw sex. She breast-balls Mark's cock before swallowing it! Gorgeous Naomi and superstud Manuel go at each other **like they haven't had sex in years.** She smothers his face before performing a back bending 69 leading to an explosive sweat-soaked climax! Even our staff agrees that we've never seen a girl move like this. 143 minutes.
>
> —Ad for the porn video *Filthy* in an Adam & Eve catalog

There's no reason, in principle, why pornography couldn't be just another harmless form of entertainment. It might even, in its own immodest way, be helpful (instruction for the clueless, relief for the dateless), life-affirming, joyous, and so on. Classical erotic art, from the lupanarium of Pompeii to the nudes of Modigliani, certainly manages to combine sexual excitement and what most people consider artistic power (who's to say that our museums aren't full of *haute pornographie*?) But, of course, porn isn't art and doesn't pretend to be.

Nobody seems to know the exact size of the American porn industry—does it take in $8 billion a year, or $10 or $14 billion?—but no one denies that it's enormous. Bourgeois folks (i.e., men) who would never darken the doorway of a porn shop don't hesitate to catch an X-rated film in their hotel rooms and charge it to their account. Porn's presence on the Internet is mind-boggling. As of July 25, 2007 googling the word "sex" produced some 434,000,000 websites (so if you spent 10 minutes on each site, it would take 8 sleepless years to exhaust just this one entry;

but then with all the shifting and expanding menus, you 'd have to start all over again).

Needless to say, righteous Republicans throughout the land have long been incensed over such erotomania. Ethically challenged Attorney General Ed Meese issued a famous 1,960 page report back in 1986 (when *Playboy* and *Penthouse* horrified right-thinking citizens with their audacious centerfolds) condemning porn and blaming it for violent crime. Alas, the Meese Crusade fell afoul of the First Amendment and did little to stem the tide (and Meese's successor, Dick Thornburgh, had to tone down an anti-pornography bill by agreeing to drop a provision of the law that would have made it a crime to possess "obscene material" on federal property—how many lecherous fish would *that* net have caught?)

Needless to say, the arrival of Bill Clinton didn't help the cause; and just when John Ashcroft was poised to drop like thunder onto the San Fernando Valley porn purveyors, 9/11 hit; and the Justice Dept. got called away. That boffo GOP danger-opportunity ideogram is still paying hefty dividends today; so there's not much chance that the DOJ will return to the fray in force any time soon.

Pornography is one of those rare issues that the right and the left (large parts of them, anyway) can agree on: Tub-thumping evangelists and orthodox radical feminists attack it for demeaning women and impugning either their Christian chastity or their natural dignity. Virtually everyone is revolted by the exploitation and sickness of "kiddie porn." And, quite apart from certifiably criminal porn, most of the rest of the stuff really is revolting.

Robotic kewpie dolls, with bulging breast implants and shaved pubes, cavort with thuggish-looking (unemployed? out on parole?) tattooed "studs" (their groins shaved as well, whether for clearer camera angles or from the industry's general aversion to body hair). Preposterous yelps of female ecstasy ("Oh yeah!") fill the air over the ground bass of wordless male groans. Frenetic, wide-eyed "nymphos" violently fellate their studly tattooed partners, as if those bulging penises contained the fountain of youth (well, they *do* contain a better-than-living wage for the ladies). Talk about cooperative: these girls like nothing better than group sex (simultaneous oral-vaginal, anal-vaginal, oral-anal-vaginal, etc. penetration), inevitably ending with the "money-shot," where the lads squirt loads of semen point-blank onto their smiling faces and into their open mouths. Man grunts in low-key satisfaction, girl glows in submissive happiness. Fade-out.

Hipper kinds of porn show men using condoms and even sensitively tossing in a few moments of cunnilingual foreplay; but the preposterous conventions of this form are seldom changed or rejected. Other beloved pornographic tropes include the fake-lesbian bacchanal (girls' night-off from strenuous servicing-the-guys) or the female-masturbation scene interrupted by a helpful male who provides what the horny little vixen *really* wants. Fans of quirkiness or the absurd might be amused by some recurrent features of both porn photos and videos: the nudes wearing Christian crosses around their necks or in their earlobes, the visible C-section scars on many of the temptresses, the suspiciously high number of mature women described as "teens" or "coeds," the *de rigueur* circumcision of male performers (talk about things the Torah never dreamed of . . .), and the universal code of categories (for the on-line shopper, etc.): Asian, Chunky, Cream Pie, Hairy (i.,e., unshaved pubic hair, with perhaps some axillary extras). Interactive, MILF (Moms I'd Like to Fuck, as almost everyone knows), Squirting, etc. Porn World is just another version of the 24/7 American Supermarket of Mind and Body, with plastic gadgets, naughty garments, creams and spices, inflatable dolls, condoms *à gogo*, whatever the heart desires.

Pornography is supposed to be anonymous (most of the X-rated actresses use *noms de querre* like Crystal Breeze, Candy Samples, Vanessa Blue, Jada Fire, while the men appear in duller disguises, such as Peter North, Rod Fontana and Mr. Marcus—but then the focus here is always on the women). And the anonymity, of course, is crucial. Pornography imagines and, to some feeble degree, realizes a utopian world of fantasy and wish-fulfillment. The pornographer, sadists aside, imagines an impossible scenario where sex causes no guilt, pain, pregnancy, or, God forbid, emotional attachment. Back in 1977 eventual *Playboy* Playmate of the Year, Patti McGuire, was quoted as saying that after a stint in L.A., she had returned to Saint Louis because (among other things) "the sex was better." Not the weather maybe or the fresh produce, but *the sex*, that indispensable, but otherwise value-free commodity.

The men in the pornographic vision are all prodigiously potent, the women all ardently and indiscriminately willing (aside from being much better looking than the men). The reality principle is suspended; life is reduced to a blissful cycle of sizzling foreplay, ecstatic coupling, and explosive orgasms, minus work, tedium or tragedy, much less that ancient male bugaboo, the "refractory period." *This* round-dance will spin on cheerily, if not happily, forever.

Still, for all its crudeness, if not evil, the stuff persists. Its survival, in fact, is assured by an unlikely coalition: of free-speech stalwarts and weak-willed voyeurs, horny teens, and flabby past-their-primers, of high-minded people afraid the suppression of porn would threaten legitimate art and low-minded people looking for distraction or masturbatory release. But there's more to it than that.

One of the most obvious things about pornography is that it's produced by and for males. Women may take an occasional curious peek at it, but it's the men and boys who subscribe to the skin magazines and stack them in the closet (or steal them from the trash). It's the men who troll the lubricious depths of the Web and rent (or buy) the trashy videos with titles like "Hand to Mouth" "Creampie Supreme," and "Tailgunners." (There's also a sub-industry of male homosexual porn, but so-called lesbian pornography is designed for the heterosexual voyeur.)

So what does all this prove? It's hardly news to women that lots of men are swine. One could always argue that porn's brainless clichés reflect and cater to the bummed-out longing of ordinary males who either wish they had more sex appeal and potency, or feel rejected (sooner or later everybody gets rejected), or lust after women way out of their league, or wonder what it would be like to . . .—or all of the above. Porn solves these problems (with images, not answers), hence its popularity.

But, whatever its psychological underpinning, the fact remains that porn *is* by and large noxious garbage, and millions of Americans can't get enough of it. And as if the vast fetid warehouses of the hard-core stuff weren't enough, there's the ongoing pornification (eroticization for dummies) of advertising, the media, and the "arts." It all suggests that America's dream of perpetual adolescence has finally come true.

Chapter 17

Mothers, Don't Let Your Daughters Grow Up to be Blondes

> She as a veil down to the slender waist
> Her unadorned golden tresses wore
> Disheveled, but in wanton ringlets waved
> As the vine curls her tendrils, which implied
> Subjection, but required with gentle sway,
> And by her yielded, by him best received,
> Yielded with coy submission, modest pride,
> And sweet reluctant amorous delay.
>
> —Milton, *Paradise Lost*, IV, 304-311

There she was, seductively draped across the cover of the November–December, 2005 issue of the *AARP* Magazine: basic black dress, wind-blown blond mane, some serious 48-year-old cleavage, *toujours gaie*, wife-mother-widow-anchorwoman, Ka-Ka-Ka-Ka-Katie Couric! Talk about a bundle of American paradoxes and absurdities: a magazine for oldsters pretending to be eternally youthful, whence the aggressively euphemistic "retired persons" and the cover girl who didn't even qualify for membership; a supposedly professional journalist vamping it up in a culture where you're either hot or you're dead, and in a country where the news has to be up-close and personal, or it gets turned off. Love that gutsy gal! Love that perky reporting! Break a leg!

O.k., so Katie may be getting a little bit long in the tooth (even as she works overtime on her gravitas), but not to worry: flick on the TV, and especially cable TV news show, like CNN's Susan Hendricks, Christi Paul, or Linda Stouffer, the latest version of that ever-popular American product, the non-threatening woman, the college-educated kewpie doll. Hey, we all know the news can be a bummer these days, what with Iraq and gas prices and the subprime mortgage sinkhole and global warming; so what better antidote than the newsbabe? (Rather than getting viewers down with scary real-world developments, she'll fill them in on handy, family-oriented advice on things like low-fat desserts, unheralded heroes, and avoiding Lyme disease.) All blondes, all the time!

But the newsbabe herself seems to be simply one more evolutionary stage in the progressive trivialization of women: since modern females insist on playing some sort of role on public life, the idea seems to be, why not draft them as cheerleaders for major male enterprises? They're easy on the eye (only the pretty, lavishly coifed ones get hired) and, if nothing else, make for an amusing change of pace. So, apart from older, more traditional vocations, such as first lady, gold star mother, pom-pom girl, babysitter, T&A advertising icon, sideline worshiper, household drudge, etc, we now see more and more women serving in the fluffier front-office bureaus of the System: as Karen-Hughes-type ambassadresses of good will, as blonde hostesses (Nancy Grace, Rita Cosby) of news shows specializing in searches for lost blondes (Elizabeth Smart, Natalee Holloway, etc.), as spokeswomen (i.e., designated liars) for tobacco, oil, or chemical companies, the White House (like the icily contemptuous Dana Perino, who not have heard about the Bay of Pigs, but will defend the indefensible all day long)—or any other criminal operation, where a deep-voiced, hard-selling guy representative might stir up resistance—and, best of all for the far right, as vigorous-venomous blonde apparatchiks (Ann Coulter, Laura Ingraham, Monica Crowley, Elizabeth Hasselbeck, etc.) defending the very institutions that have kept women imprisoned for centuries. Atta girl!

Defining the essence of All-American blondeness is made easier by recalling some of the countries more egregious non-blonde Troublemakers. A quick modern survey would suggest names like Margaret Sanger, Eleanor Roosevelt, Betty Friedan, Bella Abzug, Shirley Chisolm, Gloria Steinem, and most recently Nancy Pelosi. (Blonde Hillary Clinton used to be an honorary member of this group, thanks to her extraordinary ability to enrage already rabid conservatives; but since her election to the Senate and her campaign for president, her inner blondness seems to have taken over, as she tries more and more passionately to cuddle up with the electoral majority. Like many other women past and present, Hillary might be said to have had blondness thrust upon her.)

Americans don't mind their blonde icons showing a limited amount of independence or feistiness or spunk—witness the delicious non-stop shenanigans of Britney Spears or Paris Hilton or even (sob) Anna Nicole Smith—so long as they're basically, you know, like, on the team. To return to the cable news girls—or news readers, as the Brits more accurately call them—they're not hired to cause any disturbances with worrisome information. Sure, they *will*, when necessary, read the latest AP bulletin about scores of people blown up in Baghdad or even US Army atrocities; but their main job is to keep the audience cheerful. This means endless weather reports (ideally, rain-drenched correspondents barely able to stand up in the middle of a South Florida hurricane), clips of sporting events, celebrity gossip (from one giggling blonde to another), word of medical "breakthroughs" (can immortality be far behind?), the latest buzz about Hollywood's monster hits, inspirational tales about ordinary people "making a difference," amazing rescues, kids who care, Botox pluses and minuses, lottery winners, animal exploits, airport delays, but, above all, HELPFUL HINTS: advice from credentialed experts (some of them blonde!) to benighted laypeople on how to make their way unscathed through the mine-fields of modern life. Everything you need to know, but never would have guessed (without TV news) about child safety, mortgage rates, hot flashes, identity theft, weight loss, sunburn protection, food labeling, household germs, aging parents, you name it.

It's a lavish smorgasbord of bite-sized chunks of knowledge, gaily served up by adorable blonde waitresses, smooth-faced, smiley, chirpy, practically devoid of negatives. What more could one ask for? These women may be superficially "smart" (watch them handle that teleprompter!), but they're absolutely non-threatening. Whence the signal sent by their preference for upspeak, which turns declarative statements into hesitant questions. Its ditzy rising final intonations seem to back off from—yuck!—bald statements of fact and to beg listeners to agree with and approve the cute interlocutrice. Its robotic repetition of "like"—a silly verbal tic often afflicting males as well as females—whether as a meaningless filler or as a substitute for "said," "felt," "thought," etc., also seems to flee from boring specificity into cuddly vagueness— whence the ubiquitous tag-word "whatever." Upspeak, on or off the air, involves a lot of eye-contact, as opposed to brain-contact, if not eye-rolling and head-waggling. Watching an upspeaking newsbabe or two going at it, one inevitably thinks of Dr. Johnson's cruel, but sometimes fitting, phrase, "wretched unidea'd girls." Upspeak says: I am a child—bright-eyed, peppy, full of fun, quick on the draw, but ultimately infantile. No need to feel challenged, questioned, or, God forbid, criticized or corrected by *me*!

Some women are plainly happy to play that role; and what looks like a majority of men are equally happy to let them /make them do so. It's a lose-lose situation; or, as the newsgals themselves would probably say—for the camera anyhow, with an ingratiating flash of their pearly-whites—a win-win. We may poke some friendly fun at Blonde-Culture, but science, the axiomatic, irrefutable, foundational science of modern American life: marketing research, knows better. The name of the game is we like it like that.

Chapter 18

Up Close and Personal—Yecch

> It was in 1948 that the high point in the political button business occurred. A Pittsburgh newspaperman decided four years too early to support Dwight David Eisenhower for President. He came to A. G. [Trimble] to order buttons but couldn't think of a slogan. "Doggone it," he said, "I can't come up with a slogan, but I sure do like Ike." Answered A. G., "That's your slogan." Rich [A.G.'s son] proceeded to design the very first " I LIKE IKE" button which turned out to be the most popular political button in history.
>
> —www.agtrimble.com/about.html

Perhaps the strongest single piece of evidence for the childishness of American culture is the way we've turned political races into nonstop, media-refereed beauty contests. Despite the fact that the two major parties have more or less well-defined ideologies and positions on the issues, tens of millions of voters loudly proclaim their "independence," and wait impatiently for a candidate sexy enough to titillate their interest. During presidential campaigns the TV networks assemble focus groups of such dim-witted mugwumps, and periodically check their vital signs. (I recall one undecided citizeness who, four months into the Gore-Bush contest, stared at the camera with a look of genuine bafflement, and remarked,"Well, I've been researching all the issues; but I'm just not ready to . . ." Hey, voters are *very* careful consumers: when you're buying a long-term (a durable good, as economists like to say), big-ticket item like a President, fussiness is a virtue. And it's *so* hard to pin those wascally candidates down. Gotta think this one over a little more.

Forget such nit-picking details as war and peace, social justice, the environment, the economy, health care, immigration, Supreme Court and cabinet nominations—Americans want someone they can feel *comfortable* with. Of course, that may mean different things for different people: for the values crowd having a record unstained by Clintonesque shenanigans will be a sine qua non. Joe Six-Pack and his ilk will by definition like a candidate they'd enjoy having a beer with (no pointy-headed policy wonks, please). Any change of position will lead consistency-freaks to slap on the lethal label of "flip-flopper." Other useful characteristics include a southern accent, a presentable wife, a nondescript mainstream Protestant church affiliation, and rich but unobtrusive friends. Now if only someone could recapture the magic of Ronald Reagan.

Above all, candidates must beware the media-magnified gotcha moments: Ed Muskie's tears, Michael Dukakis' tank ride (plus his wimpish reluctance to castrate and kill Bernard Shaw's famous hypothetical attacker of Kitty), George Bush, Sr.'s glancing at his watch and his uncertainty about the price of milk, John Kerry's windsurfing, John Edwards' $400 haircut, and so on. We know what we like (soothing, *predictable* mediocrity). I LIKE IKE!

Thus the non-stop product placement, negative ads (gossip works, duh), fund-raisers, background stories, "in-depth" interviews, up-close-and-personal with the extremely personable personality featured in this week's Person of the Week/Day/Hour. Because if there's one thing we understand, it's persons—and people. We're people-persons, for cryin' out loud. And aren't people who need people the luckiest people in the world? That's why it's so important to know about the First Lady (Laddie)—we definitely didn't like what we saw of that uppity Teresa Heintz Kerry. Now impersonal stuff, like foreign policy, what to do about Iraq, Afghanistan, North Korea, Iran, Cuba, Venezuela, that's *hard* to figure out. And who knows what to think about the national debt, Social Security, the balance of payments, stem cell research, physician-assisted suicide, medical marijuana, capital punishment by lethal injection? But personal stuff, like what makes us feel safe (Rudy Giuliani with a bull horn! Dick Cheney with the Patriot Act! airport security guards with metal-detectors!), THAT we know.

It's bad enough when voters are trapped within the straitened round of their own parochial interests; but about half of Americans don't vote at all (29 million single women didn't in 2004); and many of those who do don't even know where their own interests lie, or get sidetracked from them under the influence of infantile propaganda. In effect, they vote for tax breaks they'll never see unless they win the Power Ball lottery; for corporate welfare payments to agribusiness and corporations whose stock they'll never own; for wars their children, but not those of the elected warmongers, will die in; for environmental poisons they, but not the rich, will ingest; for restrictions on their wives' and daughters' sexuality; for religious claptrap that has nothing to do with their needs or problems; and so on. As Gore Vidal said, "The genius of the American political system for 200 years lies in its giving the rich a license to steal from the poor, and making them believe they voted for it." But who cares about self-interest, enlightened or not, when you genuinely *like* the guy you vote for?

Well, of course, why not? We (fake-)personalize everything else in our culture, so why not politics? Hollywood stars and TV "personalities" are part of our imaginary extended family. We're on a pseudo-first-name basis with Leonardo and Ben and Jen and Lindsay and Brangelina and TomKat (and their babies!) and Lord knows whom else. We can't get enough Entertainment News (reporters now say "celebritology" with a semi-straight face); so why not see politics as show time? In an urban-suburban world full of strangers, it's nice to have friends, even if they happen to be as banal, inane and boring as the cast of *Friends* (or *Sex and the City*). We may not vote all that much in November, but we vote eagerly and by the tens of millions throughout the rest of the year for *American Idol* contestants and our favorite young things on the spectacularly misnamed "reality TV" shows, as we do for the players in All Star games.

Come to think of it, our ratings of professional athletes are generally more reasonable and objective than our ratings of professional politicians—we all know a good performance when we see it. (Numbers lie a lot less than sloppy impressions.) And when speaking of actual baseball, football, basketball, or hockey games, we never engage in the nonsensical sport of badmouthing the game itself, the way we do with politics, where we pretend that words like "politician" and "political" and "partisan" are somehow slimy and infra dig—shameful things that "statesmen" (are there "stateswomen"?) rise sublimely above, perhaps like that brain-numbed—but by now mythical—mediocrity, Dwight David Eisenhower. Thus, Republicans opposed, in March, 2007, to having Karl Rove testify under oath to the Senate Judiciary Committee, accused Democrats of wanting to put on a "political circus"—as if Rove himself had not been the GOP's ringmaster for most of the past decade. Our political Messiahs must come from far beyond the Beltway (no "special interests," no business as usual, no partisanship) to escape the hideous taint of "politics."

Voters routinely damn the Congress with rock-bottom approval ratings (in August 2007, they were lower than Bush's)—and then go on to reelect their beloved long-time local incumbent. But then, as the late and otherwise deservedly forgotten Senator Roman Hruska of Nebraska famously said at the Senate hearings on the domination of Nixon's doomed Supreme Court candidate, G. Harrold Carswell: "Even if he is mediocre, there are lots of mediocre judges, and people, and lawyers. They are entitled to a little representation, aren't they?" Not to worry, Roman baby. Entitled or not, they've gotten, and continue to get, all sorts of representation. We not only get the government and culture we deserve, we get the politicians and performers we like and feel oh-so-cozy with.

And that's the problem.

Chapter 19

Conservatism, Face to Face

> Conservatives get no respect . . . I can't win because I am American, white, Christian, and conservative . . . If you are a white human that loves America and happens to be a Christian, forget about it, Jack. You are the only one that doesn't have a political action committee for you . . . I mean, I was talking about it with my family yesterday. I said, "I'm tired of being the least popular person in the world" . . . "We're Americans. Nobody likes Americans. We're Americans, so the world hates us. But then inside of America, we love America—and that's becoming more and more unpopular." Being Christian is not popular anymore . . . I've got to find one thing that I agree with the rest of the world on, I guess.
>
> —Glenn Beck, on his nationally syndicated show, Apr. 2, 2007 (source: Media Matters)

One book that every liberal should own and keep ready to hand is the annual US legislative face book, *Congress at Your Fingertips* (Capitol Advantage Publishing). It contains photos (many absurdly dated) of all members of the House and Senate (plus governors and cabinet secretaries), along with chunks of vital information about them, including their education, pre-political profession, religion, marital status, years served, percentage of the vote garnered in the most recent election, and so on.

Much of the data is predictable and obtainable from other sources. It's no surprise, though worth mentioning, that all forty three members of the Congressional Black Caucus are Democrats—now that J.C. Watts, that embarrassing anomaly, has moved on to his natural calling as a lobbyist. And, speaking of embarrassment, how about the lone figure of Barack Obama in the Senate: that's not even tokenism. Anyhow, it's likewise no shock to find that of the pathetically small numbers of women in both the Senate and the House, a hefty majority are Democrats (11 out of 16, and 49 out 70, respectively). Democrats by and large have more education than Republicans, who count far more college dropouts than the majority party in the House (17 to 5—though the picture is clouded by the handful of members with only high school diplomas or A.A. degrees).

Republicans, naturally are more religious (and hypocritical) than Democrats. There's only one GOP House member, Doc Hastings of Washington, without some sort of church affiliation (apart from the one Jew, Eric Cantor of Virginia), though a suspicious number try to get away by calling themselves just "Christian," a non-existent brand in the denominational Grand Bazaar of America. Democrats have at least eight members whose faith is given as "Not Stated" (an infidel's alias, if ever there was one), plus one Buddhist (Mazie K. Hirono of Hawaii), one Muslim (Keith M. Ellison of Minnesota), and one actual self-confessed atheist (Pete Stark of California, technically signed in as a Unitarian). Right now there are just two openly gay members of Congress, Barney Frank of Massachusetts and Tammy Baldwin of Wisconsin (Baldwin lists her domestic partner, Lauren Azar—the only person in the legislative branch brave enough to do so).

Conservatives, as one might expect, draw enormous support from Mormonism, the most dim-witted and laughable major faith in America. Of the fifteen Mormons in Congress, only two, the well known Harry Reid and the utterly unknown Eni F. H. Faleomavaega of American Samoa, are Democrats. In the best misogynist tradition there isn't a single Mormon woman in Congress.

And then there are the Jews, the bulk of whom are as plainly non-observant (except for the obnoxious Joe Lieberman) as they are liberal at the rate of 28 to 1 in the House, 11 to 2 in the Senate). So we have the usual suspects lined up: blacks, women, Jews, unbelievers, gays (some overlap of necessity, here)—or, as the McCarthyites and their ilk used to say back in the fifties, the bleeding hearts.

But beyond such familiar patterns, what can one learn from *Congress at Your Fingertips*? (Hm, that title might evoke the image of a desperate citizen choking one of the many worthless individuals depicted therein.) On the level of skin-deep impressions, it's hard to miss the striking assortment of dull, complacent, blubbery, porcine faces on such Republican legislative luminaries as Chris Cannon of Utah, Rick Keller of Florida, Don Young of Alaska, or, *honoris causa*, the morally-cum-physically repugnant Gov. Hailey Barbour of Mississippi.

But, hey, to be honest, many of the Democrats aren't especially prepossessing either; and this whole method is unreliable. Still, a brief survey of a few of the stupid/barbarous positions taken or views expressed by some of the self-styled conservatives in the legislature may help to remind us what a collection of wretches Americans have voted, and continue to vote, often joyously, into office.

In alphabetical order, then, we have Sen. Tom Coburn of Oklahoma, who wants abortion providers executed and mounts fierce assaults on the "gay agenda"—and how not, since, as he himself assures us, the scourge of lesbianism has swept through some parts of Oklahoma with such devastating force that girls in public schools there are only allowed to go to the bathroom one at a time. His colleague, Jim DeMint of South Carolina is a raging fanatic (probably the most conservative in the Senate) who wants to have all 12 million illegal immigrants sent home and all openly gay persons banned from teaching in public schools. DeMint is still looking for WMDs and blames Democratic "wimps" for the casualties in Iraq. He vows to leave the Republican Party if it grants "amnesty" to illegal immigrants. Finally, there's Jim Inhofe, the irrepressible, cantankerous idiot who called global warming "the greatest hoax of the century," and who held up a large color photo of his family for the Senate to admire on June 2, 2006, noting that neither he nor his beloved wife of 47 years, nor any of twenty assembled children and grandchildren had EVER been involved in a divorce or a homosexual relationship. At the same time he blasted the "homosexual marriage lobby," equating it with the "polygamist lobby," and sternly warned that any concessions to either heinous group would lead to "unrestricted sexual conduct between adults and children, group marriage, incest, and, you know, if it feels good, do it" (Wikipedia).

In the House, conservative stalwarts include Barbara Cubin of Wyoming, a typical term-limits enthusiast who lost her enthusiasm when her time ran out. When the House was debating a bill that limited the civil liability of firearms dealers and manufacturers (H.R. 1036), this hitherto obscure political hack leapt into national exposure when she said, "I am going to tell you what. My sons are now 25 and 22, and they're blond-haired and blue-eyed. One amendment said we couldn't sell [guns] to anybody that was on drugs or had drug treatment or something like that. Well, does that mean if you go into a black community, you can't sell any gun to any black person?"

Defender of the Faith Virgil Goode of Virginia raised the alarm when Rep. Keith Ellison of Minnesota, a Muslim took his oath of office on a Koran. Unless we clamped down on immigration, Goode warned, "We will have many more Muslims in the US" (shudder). Patrick McHenry of North Carolina, an apparently closeted gay who is forever trumpeting his commitment to traditional family values, unloaded responsibility for the Mark Foley scandal squarely at the door of (whom else?) the Democrats. Marilyn Musgrave of Colorado, a resolute and successful opponent of sex education, sees gay marriage as the most important issue facing the nation. Musgrave has also won the endorsement of the KKK. Viewers of *Borat* will recall Charles "Chip" Pickering, Jr. of Mississippi, who made a cameo appearance attacking evolution and leading a palpably phony mob of born-againers shouting and jiving at a prayer meeting.

But perhaps the most depressing fact about the brainless tribe of conservatives is the number of members all but unknown outside their district who proudly vote the wrong way on every issue, year in, year out. Take Rep. Lamar Smith, Republican from Texas, now in his eleventh term who has voted as follows:

- No to embryonic cell research
- Yes to funding health-care providers who won't mention abortion
- Yes to a Constitutional amendment banning same-sex marriage
- Yes to a Constitutional amendment banning flag desecration
- Yes to making the Patriot Act permanent
- No to allowing stockholders to vote on executive compensation
- Yes to replacing illegal export tax breaks with $140 billion in new breaks
- No to funding alternative sentencing instead of more prisons
- Yes to making federal death penalty appeals harder
- Yes to prohibiting needle exchange and medical marijuana
- Yes to allowing school prayer during "War on Terror"
- Yes to give federal aid only to schools allowing voluntary prayer
- No to the moratorium on drilling for oil offshore

- No to start implementing the Kyoto Protocol
- No to prohibiting oil drilling in the Arctic National Wildlife Refuge
- Yes to cutting back on critical habitat for endangered species
- Yes to speed up forest-thinning projects
- No to granting Washington DC an electoral vote and vote in Congress
- No to protecting whistle-blowers from employer recrimination
- Yes to requiring photo ID for voting in federal elections
- Yes to prohibiting suing gun-makers and sellers for gun misuse
- Yes to decreasing gun waiting period from three days to one
- Yes to limited prescription drug benefit for Medicare recipients
- No to requiring negotiated prescription prices for Medicare part D
- Yes to ban physician-assisted suicide
- Yes to allowing electronic surveillance without a warrant
- Yes to continuing intelligence gathering without civil oversight
- Yes to building a fence along the Mexican border
- No to restrict employer interference in union organizing
- Yes to making Bush tax cuts permanent
- Yes to eliminate the estate tax
- Yes to increase fines for indecent broadcasting
- No to redeploying US troops out of Iraq, starting in 90 days.

—www.ontheissues.org

Tom Tancredo rounds out the team, perhaps the most (recently) notorious Congressional nutcase, for saying that Miami had become a Third World country and that bombing Mecca might be called for. Tancredo is a leader of the immigration xenophobes, and is on record for claiming that the day Rove v. Wade is repealed would be the greatest day in the country's history.

Well, the list could be extended, and surely will, as time passes, and new monsters arrive to replace the old ones. Of course, every country, like every clan, has its lunatics; but these characters from Congress are famous and powerful; *and no one questions their sanity*. They occasionally lose elections, but mostly they win them (*Congress at Your Fingertips* also tells you how many terms the politicians have had, and how handily they won their last election. As everyone knows, incumbents tend to sail through time after time.) And this, evidently, is the best the country, God help it, can do.

Chapter 20

Culture is So Over

> Insofar as multiculturalism means a wide choice of personal identities or "lifestyles"—shifting, temporary, overlapping—it faces scarcely any significant opposition in the United States at the beginning of the millennium. The multiculturalism of strong ethnic values and group solidarity maintained heroically against the pressures of a Eurocentric majority, on the other hand, is as dead in the real world as the nineteenth-century anthropology that gave rise to its basic concepts. In the university and elsewhere, this sort of multiculturalism represents the nostalgia of the left for an older world, the exact counterpart of conservative nostalgia for a small-town, Christian, pre-New Deal America that vanished long ago down the same historical drain.
>
> —Christopher Clausen, *Faded Mosaic:*
> *The Emergence of Post-Cultural America* (2000)

If, as Nathan Glazer told us, we're all multi-culturalists now, nobody is more multicultural than American academics; and nowhere is the mantra of diversity chanted with more rapt piety than on college campuses. But rapturous devotion is a poor substitute for reason.

Having made the unsettling discovering that the literary canon reflects the biases and blind spots of the past, earnest revisionists are now thrilled to find that minor works by women-writers, such as Kate Chopin's *The Awakening*, are mighty neglected masterpieces. So-so writers who happen to be both black and female, like Toni Morrison, are positively deified. (The Swedes took our word for it and gave her a Nobel—but then the list of Nobel Prize winners for Literature is studded with names like Wladyslaw Reymont, Erik Axel Karlfeldt, Frans Emil Sillanpää, and Grazia Deldedda.) Academic dogma declares that all things postcolonial are automatically precious (life in present-day Zimbabwe?), even as all things colonial are per se evil (the ban on suttee?) Card-carrying liberals who vehemently scorn fundamentalist Jesus-shouters piously exalt picturesque primitive practices like the Mexican food offerings left on graves for el Día de los Muertos. Feminists who wage a just war on western sexism somehow forget to mention the horrors of 130 million African clitoridectomies. Professors rightly indignant over Abu Ghraib and Guantánamo listen without objection to Muslim speakers uttering palpable nonsense about jihad as "spiritual struggle," about the profound Islamic respect for women, or the literally divine inspiration of the Qur'an.

Often enough, as I have seen in my own disciplinary neighborhood, administrators who never stop preaching about excellence and high standards are perfectly willing to ignore both and hire incompetent Third-World or minority candidates to win Affirmative Action brownie points. And if it takes higher salaries to win such recruits away from competing institutions, so be it. Where's that socially transforming checkbook?

Now the New Comrades Ashram will surely do no more harm than the Old Boy Network, which it's replacing. But, apart from some glaring instance of silliness (the San Francisco school board's 1998 ukase prescribing that half of all authors on its reading list be non-white, i.e., any color or combination of colors except white, regardless of literary quality), the larger issue that emerges here is the naive idealization and sentimentalization of culture *tout court*. Culture, or non-western cultures at any rate, is increasingly viewed as beautiful and endangered, like pandas and blue whales , and hence sacred.

But, of course, culture is *not* sacred, not even the Tibetan culture currently slated for extinction at the hands of Chinese communist invaders. Culture is just a more or less coherent amalgam of customs, attitudes, and structures of control. As it evolves over time, it may create some traditions that are truly worth keeping, as in the rule of law and other restraints on arbitrary power. But given the monstrous record of culturally approved violence, oppression, and lunacy, the omnipresent culturally enshrined social injustice, sexism, cruelty to animals, and ecological havoc, *everything* cultures do has to be subject to permanent, suspicious scrutiny; and the criterion for keeping or changing any cultural artifact has to be pragmatic reason, not the culture itself.

In fact, as Christopher Clausen argues persuasively in *Faded Mosaic*, culture in the sense of a supremely authoritative body of norms is dead in America (and moribund elsewhere in the First World). The chaotic mass individualism that Clausen sees as having taken its place may not be—is not in fact—pretty; but there's no going back. People who talk, or dream, about connecting with their "roots" aren't rediscovering a lost cultural identity. They're simply making some emotional purchases in the Supermarket of Myths: most of them settle for cuisine—and how much of THAT comes to the table, of home or restaurant, without literal or figurative blood on it?—a few others buy their way back completely into a disused family religion, and fewer still actually end up speaking their forgotten *mame-loshen*. But *they*'re the ones picking and choosing, not the Tribe, or the Ancestors, or the Great Spirit. So, we're talking about interior decoration for the mind, or do-it-yourself home repairs for the soul.

It's true that professional ethnics, such as some professors of the Humanities or Social Sciences, have gone way beyond the amateurish identity politics of lay practitioners. They may even belong, heart, soul, and tongue, to the culture that they're proselytizing for in the classroom. But, to the extent that any of this goes beyond sheer intellectual enthusiasm and esthetic gusto, they're inhabiting the fogbound world of sentimental multiculturalism—check with your local provider of "Afro-centric" education, courses on "native Americans" taught by whites, or—on bad days—almost anything with the word "Studies" after it. Academics who should know better blithely assume that culture is good, so long as it's not American culture, and hence the more cultures, the better.

For every political action, there is, or can be, an equally stupid opposite reaction. The strident blasts of the America-firsters, reveling in limitless opportunities for bluster supplied by the War on Terror, have provoked a propagandistic hardening by orthodox leftists. Consider the following excerpt from a rant by Alexander Cockburn (dated December 4, 2006 and entitled "When Will Kristoff" (sic, casually misspelling the name of *The New York Times'* Nicholas Kristof) "Go to the Occupied Territories?"): "As a zone of ongoing, large-scale bloodletting Darfur in the western Sudan has big appeal for US news editors. Americans are not doing the killing, or paying for others to do it. So there's no need to minimize the vast slaughter with the usual drizzle of 'allegations.' There's no political risk here in sounding off about genocide in Darfur. The crisis in Darfur is also very photogenic."

Hm, we wouldn't want to suggest that Third World countries could ever commit terrible crimes, now would we? That's a western monopoly. Attacking Hosni Mubarak is o.k., since Washington props up his repressive regime; but there's no need to mention the monstrous behavior of Libya's Muammar al-Qadaffi, Sudan's Umar Hassan Ahmad al-Bashir (who was deeply disturbed by a fifteen-minute Dutch video attacking the Qur'an, though not so much by the fact nearly half a million blacks have been massacred in his own country by the Arab Janjaweed), Nigeria's Olusegun Obasanjo, Guinea's Teodoro Obango Nguema Mbasago, or Zimbabwe's Robert Mugabe. The Organization of African Unity scarcely dares to raise its feeble voice to criticize them, so how could we tainted white outsiders? Other dictators, such as Kim Jong Il (arguably a worse person than Dick Cheney), Kazakhstan's Nursultan Nazarbayev, Myanmar's military junta, or Belarus's Alexander Lukashenko are passed over in silence by leftist multicultural fans: Criticizing them might smack of colonialism, racism, hegemonism, militarism, yadda-yadda-yadda. And God forbid one suggests that the Palestinians are as error-prone as the Israelis: say *that*, and the ghost of Edward Said will arise and throw rocks at you.

Still deeper than the silliness of American multiculturalists' mechanical distribution of warm fuzzies for the Third World and cold contempt for individualistic, rationalistic First World elites lies their blindness to the ecological catastrophe being wrought by *all* cultures. They may condemn the destructive wasteful, polluting, energy-addicted behavior of the West, but what about the mindless natalism of Muslim and Hindu cultures? The horrific treatment of animals in Asia and Africa? Galloping ecocide in communist China?

At the bottom of this foggy-mindedness seem to lie primitivist fantasies about the innocence of a human nature not yet corrupted by the vices of capitalist civilization. Forget about the selfish gene or our lupine behavior (a slander against wolves). It's the old idealized Marxist proletariat, the muscular peasants of Stalinist and Maoist poster art, in a new, naive ecumenical package, a religion for the otherwise religionless academics, "activists," publishers, pundits, and other uncritical American fools. What a bore.

Chapter 21

Wigger Nation

> I saw the best minds of my generation destroyed by madness, starving hysterical naked, dragging themselves through the negro streets at dawn looking for an angry fix, angelheaded hipsters burning for the ancient heavenly connection to the starry dynamo in the machinery of night . . .
>
> —Alan Ginsburg, *Howl*

> African-American teenagers are beset on all sides by dangerous myths about race. The most poisonous one defines middle-class normalcy and achievement as "white," while embracing violence, illiteracy and drug dealing as "authentically" black. This fiction rears its head from time to time in films and literature. But it finds its most virulent expression in rap music, which started out with a broad palette of themes but has increasingly evolved into a medium for worshiping misogyny, materialism and murder.
>
> —Brent Staples, "How Hip-Hop Lost its Way and Betrayed its Fans," *New York Times*, May 12, 2005

America's love-hate relation with black culture is a strange story. In *On the Road* (1957) Jack Kerouac describes himself wandering through the streets of Denver, wishing he were "a Negro"—a wish realized four years later by John Howard Griffin in *Black Like Me*. In point of fact, it's a common American fantasy. As far back as 1828 a man named Thomas Dartmouth Rice blackened his face and did a song and dance routine ominously named *Jim Crow*. In 1843 the first minstrel show opened, and in 1848, inspired by the Christy Minstrels, Stephen Foster began writing his famous quasi-Negro melodies. Nobody thought it strange when a Jew named Al Jolson (Asa Yoelson), who was born in Russia and wanted to be a cantor, belted out "Mammy" for the first time in 1909. And for decades (1928-1960) millions of complacent whites listened to the radio antics of "Amos 'n' Andy," whose laughable black protagonists were played by two whites, Freeman Gosden and Charles Correll. Such entertainment has often (and justly) been described as racist—though it reached the sublime at least once, in Gershwin's *Porgy and Bess* (1935)—but it also reflects the fascination and envy that black life arouses in the white American.

Nowadays, of course, the media, if not the centers of political and economic power, are awash with images of blacks. At least since the '80s blacks have been a potent presence on TV, starting with Bryant Gumbel in the morning to Oprah Winfrey in the afternoon, to Arsenio Hall at night. Only Oprah is still a major presence now, but there are plenty of bright up-and-coming replacements: Russ Mitchell, Tony Harris, and Jason Carroll—just to mention the news business. Blacks dominate America's most fervently believed national religion, sports, as much as ever—actually more than ever, now that so many people have cable. Blacks steal the show, from comedy (Eddie Murphy) to drama (Morgan Freeman, Samuel L. Jackson, Denzel Washington, Halle Berry, Jennifer Hudson, Jamie Foxx, Forest Whitaker, etc.) to politics (Barack Obama). Blacks now fill such archetypal roles as father figure (Bill Cosby), Miss America, Secretary of State, presidential candidate and so on.

But perhaps the most startling recent feature of this process has been the emergence of wiggers, the white groupies of black culture. If for some reason you've missed this development, just watch the teenagers, especially the boys, emerging from any school bus—hip-hoppers everywhere, from the backwards baseball caps (see Chapter 10, "Hats Off, Guys") to the thigh-length T-shirts to the baggy pants to the rhapsodies on "niggaz" and "hoes" wafting through their iPods.

There are lots of reasons for the hold blacks have on the white imagination, but perhaps the key to it can be traced back to that subversive classic *Huckleberry Finn* (1884). In Twain's astonishingly radical (and negative) vision of America the only complete person is Jim, an illiterate runaway slave, whose moral decency occasionally borders on sentimental perfection. To this day, when whites (some of them, anyway) look at blacks, they can't help suspecting that blacks are more alive than they are (not to mention the persistence, in the vast and not-very-far underground of white-controlled pornography, of the Supermasculine Black Buck) or, worse yet, that blacks are—by and large—the only ones with "soul." But, of course, if you don't have soul, you're not really human.

That sounds like an alarming thesis, but consider the following invidious comparisons, beginning some decades ago and working up into the present: Muhummad Ali vs. Gerry Cooney, Bessie Smith vs. Kate Smith, Bill White vs. Phil Rizzuto, Willie Brown vs. Charles Grassley, Flo-Jo Griffith and Jackie Joyner vs. Billie-Jean King and Chris Evert, James Earl Jones vs. Ernest Borgnine, Marvin Gaye vs. Steve Lawrence, B.B. King vs. Pat Boone, Queen Latifah vs Ellen Degeneres, Jamie Foxx vs. Ben Stiller, Beyoncé vs. Andie MacDowell, Donna Brazille vs. Mary Matalin, Dave Chapelle vs. Dave Letterman, Lebron James vs. Adam Morrison. You could even play this game with scoundrels or shady characters: Adam Clayton Powell vs. Spiro Agnew, Eldridge Cleaver vs. Charles Colson, Rev. Creflo Dollar vs. Rev. Jim Bakker, Dennis Rodman vs. Ilie Nastasie, Tupac Shakur vs. Pete Doherty.

The names speak for themselves: the blacks in question have, or had, style, pizzazz, vitality, elegance, oomph, brilliance, bite. Their white counterparts have . . . well, let's just say there's a believable stereotype of whites as flabby, stodgy, square, slow, flat, boring. Whites are notorious for not having rhythm, for using the backboard instead of slam-dunking, for going by the book. They can't help themselves. While blacks are at home in their bodies, whites are often not on speaking terms with theirs. Black English has verve, white English is stilted. Black athletes come through in the clutch, white athletes choke. Blacks behave spontaneously and naturally, whites strain as if to follow some distant teleprompter.

Of course, these *are* stereotypes, but you can't dismiss them as nonsense. Surely whites would never have persecuted blacks so relentlessly if they hadn't felt threatened by them and envious of them. From the first, white racism wasn't blind hostility, but a love-hate relationship. In *Robinson Crusoe* (1719) Friday is demeaned as childish, ignorant, a born slave. On the other hand, he's also a splendid physical specimen, phenomenally quick, and a better Christian than his "master." Crusoe insists on Friday's speaking English, and never even bothers to ask him his real name; but it's clear that, once he has saved Friday from becoming an entree in a cannibal feast, he needs Friday more than Friday needs him. The master always does.

From the perspective of white civilization, blacks are the outsiders, the Other. (The most dramatic, not to say hysterical, contemporary myth expressing this notion is *King Kong*, the story of the ultimate, though fundamentally benign, black savage.) The Other is a curious creature, a sort of reversed self-image. Whites see blacks as everything they themselves aren't—vibrant, unselfconscious, sexually free, full of animal grace, members of an uproarious exotic tribe. Of course, for many whites these positives are more than matched by a host of negatives, which we find summed up in the familiar racist caricatures of blacks as stupid, shiftless, dirty, etc.

Caricatures, in fact, were the key to the minstrel show—blacks as bug-eyed jesters, with toothy grins, swaggering walks, and Sambo humor. And caricatures have continued to be whites' basic mode of portraying blacks. But that's not surprising (we may wonder, pessimistically, whether any race will ever see another race without weird distortions; it seems more likely that the races will first have to get so totally shuffled and mixed that race itself will mean less and less to anyone—a process that is actually well under way). The funny thing is how much admiration, begrudging or frank, lies beneath the scorn. (Whereas blacks don't put on white-faced musicales: Who would bother to come?)

And so the irony persists: in a country where being black carries with it a grim legacy of hatred and oppression, the oppressors (or their descendants or the heirs to their wealth) often walk around wishing they could be like the oppressed. In the 1960s black politicians began fighting the inferiority complex of some of their own people with the slogan, "Black is beautiful." No doubt that was a message both blacks and whites needed to get. But, curiously enough, a great many white people, even the racists, had gotten it long before.

Still, there are problems. Black American culture, whether in its plain statistical reality or in its hyped commercialized edition, is a dubious model. Rates of dropping out of school, unemployment, drug addiction, STDs, alcoholism, broken families, illegitimacy, domestic violence, incarceration, etc. are horribly high. No doubt poverty and racism explain most of this misery, but knowing that doesn't change the grim facts. And those facts, instead of spawning an immense popular literature of protest, go widely ignored, even as hip-hop artists (to the deafening applause of their camp followers, black and white) revel on a mythic stage of frenzied machismo. The firing of Don Imus from MSNBC for his "nappy-headed ho's" remark sparked some indignation at brutal rap lyrics, but little has changed. The wellsprings of black humanity may be as deep and rich as ever, but don't look to see that reflected in the offerings of the Black Entertainment cable network, which perfectly match the banality and predictability of their white counterparts.

Indeed, BET might well be seen as *worse*, with more racial caricatures than Bill Cosby could shake a stick at: thuggish-looking men canoodling with sluttish-looking women, music videos featuring nothing but prodigious ripples of bling and boobs. It's the Pimpmobile Express speeding down a sky-high fast lane, driven by tattooed clowns with silly names like Notorius B.I.G., Jeru the Damaga, and Kool Moe Dee.

Nearly a century and a half after the Emancipation Proclamation, blacks are still a long way from freedom; and, hideous as the white man's role in this has been, it's not all his fault. Here as elsewhere on the American scene, the safest generalization seems to be: What a Mess.

Chapter 22

American Catholics and Other Bright Lights

> Therefore let it be said that the titanic conflict between Light and Darkness, theism and atheism, is an all-out, total war. The rules of engagement are similar to the wars unto death we read about in the Old Testament between the Israelites and some of their enemies who were placed under the ban, the decree of absolute annihilation. Let it be said loud and clear: There can be no "ecumenical dialog" between theism and atheism! Mixing elements of the naturalistic origins story into the theistic origins story is like putting arsenic into koolaid to produce a Jonestown cocktail. There can be no compromise between the theistic and naturalistic origins stories, no synthesis of the two. Among theists there should develop a common sense consensus that any attempt to accommodate the naturalistic origins story into the theistic origins story should be branded Anathema.
>
> —Fr. David R. Becker, "Evolution and Revisionist Catholicism," kolbecenter.org/becker.revcath.html

Even as the rest of the world looks on in contemptuous disbelief, a clear majority of Americans refuse to believe in evolution (it's just a theory, right?—i.e., an "idea" wandering around in the no man's land between the now exploded possibility that the moon is made of green cheese and the utter certainty that Tiger Woods is the best golfer on earth). Our Ivy League A.B. and M.B.A. President has long since declared his support for teaching Intelligent Design in the classroom alongside Darwinism. Hey, why not?

Meanwhile, many, probably most, American believers continue to assume that there's no essential conflict between faith and science. We have, after all, hundreds of religiously affiliated colleges and universities, where science is taught by (one hopes) professionally qualified men and women, whose classrooms and laboratories are seldom if ever invaded by devout screaming Luddites. Peaceful coexistence, no big deal, right?

It's true, one could fashion a satirical thought-experiment about the possibility of blending, instead of segregating, the realms of sacred and secular truth, for example in the case of the largest and most clearly-dogmatically defined religious group in America, the Roman Catholic Church, along lines like this:

- *Catholic Anthropology*—asks why Jews, though unbelievers, are smarter than Catholics; decides all worthwhile people are "anonymous Catholics";
- *Catholic Astronomy*—concedes that Galileo may have had a point after all, sort of; offers belated apology for condemnation;
- *Catholic Biology*—grounds ontological inferiority of females; studies and celebrates parthenogenesis;
- *Catholic Chemistry*—proves evil of the Pill; defines molecular structure of holy water;
- *Catholic Geography*—maps imaginary regions of sacred space: Heaven, Purgatory, and Hell; explains disappearance of Limbo;
- *Catholic History*—refutes seeming fallibility of Popes and ugly mistakes by Church;
- *Catholic Linguistics*—untangles nonsensical statements in papal encyclicals;
- *Catholic Material Sciences*—explains why communion hosts, despite being Jesus' body and blood, taste like matzos ;
- *Catholic Mathematics*—establishes that $1 + 1 + 1 = 1$; urges "Increase and Multiply!"
- *Catholic Physics*—studies suspension of laws of gravity at Ascension, Assumption, etc.
- *Catholic Psychology*—traces soul to the pineal gland; rehabilitates make-believe;

- *Catholic Sexology*—explores perils of masturbation, fornication, and same-sex marriage; validates supreme grandeur of celibacy;

Well, you get the idea. Actually, when I was a lad in parochial schools, a half-century ago, we were told that there was no conflict between science and religion. They were separate, but equal spheres—wait, not that; rather, Truth was One, so there couldn't, in principle, be any contradictions in the big, wide, wonderful world of Creation. Catholics, American and otherwise, traditionally had limited interest in Scripture (which raises all sorts of sticky can-you-believe-this? questions); and I remember feeling contempt for silly Protestants who wouldn't accept evolution. The danger facing Catholic students at secular colleges (and this was why we weren't supposed to go there) came not from science professors, but from the sneaky, seductive philosophy profs who could trip up guileless Catholic underclassmen with their eerily plausible atheistic refutations of St. Thomas's proofs for the existence of God. (Once armed with the breastplate of Neo-Scholasticism, young Catholics could supposedly face Humean or Nietzschean slings and arrows unperturbed.)

In the 21st century this irenic view of science is still the standard orthodox view outside the fundamentalist lunatic-fringe; but it suffers from serious problems. These are best summed up in a go-for-the-jugular formula from Hume's *Inquiry Concerning Human Understanding* (1748): "If we take in hand any volume of Divinity, or school [i.e., medieval scholastic] metaphysics, for instance, let us, ask, *Does it contain any abstract reasoning concerning quantity or number?* No. *Does it contain any experimental reasoning concerning matter of fact and existence?* No. Commit it then to the flames; for it can contain nothing but sophistry and illusion." By definition religious statements have nothing to say about quantity or number, nor do they deal with "experimental reasoning," in that they can never be falsified by any sort of scientific test. Not only will a million CAT scans never find the soul nor space shuttles ever dock in heaven (though some Mormons point to Kolob, a star supposedly right next to the throne of God), but no true believer will ever accept any evidence purporting to disprove his or her faith—unlike, for example, the Dalai Lama who has said that if science disproves any tenet of Buddhism, the tenet will simply have to go.

What this comes down to is compartmentalization (what the Germans call *Abschottung*), the time-tested strategy, now quasi-triumphant in America, of walling-off and water-proofing vulnerable rooms in our mental mansions out of the highly justified anxiety that they might collapse under pressure from the tsunami of empirical facts. Most people take the weekend off from work and an hour or so on Friday, Saturday, or Sunday off from reality and logic. (Just because Christopher Hitchens says the same thing doesn't mean it isn't so.)

And the reason is simple. Once upon a time religion did a lot more than enshrine a carefully delimited creed (half a page or so), code (some key thou-shalt-nots), and cult (a place to go and things to do at 11 a.m. on Sunday). It used to include cosmology (at least in the form of powerful, if unreliable, origin myths), metaphysics (at a time when practically everyone believed there was a vast world *meta-ta-physika*, beyond the coarse-grained physical-natural phenomena that we're up to our ears in), history (practically none of the events recounted in the Bible can be found in any other source), eschatology (the pseudo-science describing how the world will end, still widely accepted in the red states), political and personal ethics, and so on.

But, as we know, centuries of development, not to say progress, in those and other areas have whacked and whittled away at the "deposit of faith" until, like the Papal States, it has been reduced to a symbolic vestigial kingdom, like the Vatican's 109 acres, which is just about the size of my own college campus. And, once more like Vatican City, it's not a place that many people actually live in; it's a splendid tourist attraction, revered and deeply loved, but when all is said and done insubstantial.

Which doesn't stop American believers, so proudly different from European secularists, from raving about it and seeing it as infinitely bigger than it really is. And to do that, one need simply peer through the magnifying glass of faith. In the Bible "faith" (Heb. *emuna*, Grk. *pistis*) seems to mean something more like trust, e.g., Abraham makes contact, through a series of visitations from a mysterious, powerful god whose spectacular promises Abraham (originally called Abram until God makes over his identity) trusts, presumably because, apart from the jolts of contact he's already gotten in the theophanies, God has already delivered handsomely by facilitating the quasi-impossible birth of Isaac.

But with modern believers(which means, among other things, every single serious US presidential candidate now and for the foreseeable future), it's not so much a question of trusting that mysterious Friend—whom the vast majority of them haven't even imagined meeting—but of the familiar act of mental gymnastics: leaping over the void of concrete experience into the happy Never-never-land of religious conviction. More crudely put, faith is what Mark Twain called "believing what you know ain't so" (*Pudd'nhead Wilson's New Calendar*) and what Ambrose Bierce, in a still more negative vein, defined as "belief without evidence in what is told by one who speaks without knowledge of things without parallel" (*The Devil's Dictionary*). One trusts, ultimately, out of love; one believes because a) it feels good, and b) it's a sin not to. But Americans don't like that kind of talk. (And, wait a minute, isn't Mark Twain part of Disney World?)

And so they believe, or at least they say they do. But where faith-as-hobby seldom causes any trouble (every now and then the courts have to force Christian Science parents to let their sick children be operated on), faith-as-lobby is something else. Promoters of "faith-based initiatives" want to fill church coffers and strong-arm needy non-believers. Others want to decorate government space with the images of Ten Commandments and Jesus, whether in the cradle or on the cross. And, of course, aggressive Christians campaign to ban abortion, squash stem cell research, demonize gays, and censor the air waves in the name of faith. This tide may ebb when the nation's most celebrated born-again sinner returns to private life; but then again it may not. As Schiller said, "against stupidity the gods themselves fight in vain." And, as Einstein said, "the difference between genius and stupidity is that genius has its limits."

In any case the bald statistical fact that belief tends to shrink with scientific (or humanistic) education and to swell among drop-outs and the uninformed doesn't carry much weight in a society that likes to think of itself as egalitarian. (Well, we admit the proverbial "rocket scientists" into a quasi-supernatural elite, but who's ever met one of those?) Imagine the sensational buzz if a "creation scientist" ever won a Nobel Prize; only that's not going to happen (blind cliquish bias, of course). Meantime, the fate of Bible Belt obscurantists, like that of old-time Catholics, begins to bear an eerie resemblance to that of the polar bears: as the planet heats up (with accurate information, as with greenhouse gases), they'll find their former habitat melting away, with desperate and possibly hideous consequences. But by then, we'll probably all be cooked anyway.

Chapter 23

Sexual Wisdom from the Horse's Ass

Frequently Asked Questions:
Is it okay for a man to dress like a woman?

This is one of those issues that the Lord decided to directly address in His Word. Deuteronomy 22:5 says, "A woman must not wear men's clothing, nor a man wear women's clothing, for the Lord your God detests anyone who does this." God made you to be the person He wanted you to be. A man is to live, dress, act and look like a man—the way God intended.

Be sure that you realize, though, that God condemned the act of cross-dressing; but, even though He knew you would struggle with this, He loved you so much that He sent His Son to die for you. That kind of love has power that can help you overcome any sin in your life. God wants to help you gain control of this issue. This is what God says about temptation: "No temptation has seized you except what is common to man. And God is faithful; he will not let you be tempted beyond what you can bear. But when you are tempted, he will also provide a way out so that you can stand up under it."

—www.raptureready.com

One of the weirder things about America is the way the clergy dispense apodictic rules and super-confident advice on sex. *They* know (*they* say *they* know, *they* think *they* know) what the layfolk should and shouldn't do in that department, and *they* never shut up about it. This is more than a little strange, insofar as the Bible has almost nothing of value to say on the subject.

Marriage in the Bible is basically a form of male ownership. Biblical adultery occurs when a wife sleeps with any man other than her husband-master [*ba'al, kyrios*], *not* when a husband sleeps with an unmarried [coitally unowned] woman. Wives are supposed to be humble and submissive. Female fertility is good, we are repeatedly told in Holy Writ, which pities and looks down on the sterile woman (the Bible attributes *all* cases of "barrenness" to women). Having boys is better than having girls, who often go unnamed in the Bible (starting with Noah's wife and daughters-in-law); and every single biblical woman who initially has trouble conceiving (from Sarah to Rebekah to Rachel to Samson's (unnamed) mother to Hannah to Elizabeth to Mary) gives birth to a boy. Lust is more or less unavoidable, so get it out of your system, and move on to more important things. Not content with embracing Judaism's rich misogynistic heritage, Christianity went one step further and preached the lunatic cult of virginity.

And now, of course, there's no limit to the nonsense coming our way from America's Bible-belters. On March 18, 2007 the Washington Post reported the latest controversial utterances by the Rev. R. Albert Mohler Jr., a spokesman for the mighty (16 million members) Southern Baptist Convention. Mohler had already caused a stir by suggesting that a) homosexuality *might* after all be genetically determined—as opposed to the usual fundamentalist dogma that it's a whoop-de-do "lifestyle" option—but that b) it was *still* a sin anyway. That riled both the conservatives and the liberals; but then Mohler stirred up still more fury by suggesting that if gayness were genetic, it might be possible to head the problem off at the pass, so to speak, by applying a potent biochemical patch to the bellies of pregnant women to nip that evil gene in the bud. As always, know-nothings have no objection against enlisting the aid of "science" to combat Satan. Stay tuned for further can-you-top-this developments.

Of course, all the power and prestige that ministers, priests, and (to a lesser extent) rabbis have wielded and enjoyed in this highly charged territory has come with a price: heightened expectations from the rank and file of better-than-average behavior on the part of their pulpit-dwelling guides and gurus. And, no doubt with a certain malice, the secular Fourth Estate keeps reporting stories of sexual straying by godly reverends, from the tale of Jim Bakker and Jessica Hahn, to Jimmy Swaggart, (who was busy hounding his adulterous clerical colleague, the Rev. Albert

Gorman, before he fell prey to the charms of Debra Murphee) up to the fall of Pastor Ted Haggard, who has by now been certified as 100% free of his old Sodomitical hankerings after a period of—what else?—rehab.

Actually, at this point it's only fair to mention the often-ignored fact that the priestly-ministerial office is itself erotically charged, so being struck by libidinal thunderbolts is a nearly inevitable occupational hazard. Apart from the countless juicy opportunities afforded by private counseling sessions, the very act of condemning the sins of the flesh, real or imagined, which preachers spend so much of their time doing, occurs in a sexually stereotyped environment: the booming-voiced, vehement male minister haranguing his passive (and, ideally, fascinated) audience, which, in the case of Christians, likely contains more women than men.

Priests and preachers of whatever denomination serve as intermediaries between God and humanity, an intrinsically "sexy" function. They dwell in a sort of electrically charged middle space between heaven and earth—whether the traditional raised pulpit or the more modest podium. They attract and diffuse divine energy, like lightning rods. All the qualities generally associated with masculinity—authority, power, decisiveness, strictness, know-how, etc.—can be found in abundance among the clergy. Recall the brooding, majestically bearded figure of Michelangelo's Moses or even (since Christ too is a priest, see the Letter to the Hebrews 4.14ff.) the awesomely masculine, if not ferocious, Christ the Pantocrator staring down at us from the domes of Byzantine churches. No surprise, then, that many leading American ministers are thoroughly virile types—and that some of them have a hard time controlling themselves when attractive parishioners or altar-boys come their way. Though it may be the height of political incorrectness to link Muhammad and his nine wives to Brigham Young and his twenty-nine, much less to wacko religious phallocrats like Jim Jones and David Koresh, the stubborn fact remains: prophets (if they want them) get lots of girls.

Which helps to explain why they have so much to say to *us* about sex. The Bible knows all about a number of interesting subjects like circumcision (an early version of the pre-redeemed Chuck Colsen's logion that, "When you have them by the balls, their hearts and minds will follow"), menstruation and other forms of feminine "uncleanness," the presence or absence of hymenal bleedings on the wedding night (once a capital offense), the liturgical status of eunuchs, etc. Oddly enough, there's no mention of a wedding ceremony (because it didn't exist) in the Bible nor of the later sacrament of marriage (ditto). And there are other odd silences: the Hebrew Bible has never heard about lesbianism, and neither Testament says a word about masturbation (Onan was practicing coitus interruptus, not "self-abuse").

But not to worry: later generations of imaginative Jesus-screaming commentators have filled in all the gaps; and their epigones can now walk you through any area of sexual conduct, however murky or confusing, fortified with reams of regulations and commentary. Above all, in these newly conservative times American evangelical clergy can prod us all to sexual virtue. They replace sex ed with abstinence education. They create programs with names like "True Love Waits" (with TLW rings, bracelets, watches and pins to remind susceptible teen virgins of their solemn vow of celibacy). They churn out tapes with titles like "Passport to Purity." (Studies show none of this works; but, never mind—it's the thought that counts.) They promote brainwashing camps, like "Refuge," run by Love in Action International in Memphis, Tennessee, to wean adolescents from the ever-threatening gay lifestyle. As always, they celebrate the extreme godliness (in principle) of heterosexuality and execrate the hell-bound swinishness of homosexuality. Any questions? Click on thepurebed.com, where Pastor Joe Beam can answer them all (the good news here is that since the Bible has almost nothing to say about sexual techniques, Christian couples can generally take silence for consent on issues like oral sex, anal sex, mutual masturbation, etc., so long as they steer clear of the obvious moral shoals: adultery, group sex, incest, and pornography-as-stimulant). What about intercourse during menstruation? gotquestions?org will guide you through that one (true, Leviticus 21.18 comes down very hard on it, but, hey, much of the Old Testament is now obsolete, so on the off-chance that the little lady doesn't mind . . .)

Elsewhere Christian groups and their reverend spokesmen lead the crusade against abortion (undeterred by the awkward fact that nowhere does the Bible equate a fetus with a person), with its prayer vigils (where ecstatically communing-with-the-Lord activists duct-tape their mouths in a "silent scream"), protest marches, picketing of Planned Parenthood clinics, and the occasional, but attention-getting murder of abortion-providers. "Sancta simplicitas!" cried the Czech Protestant leader Jan Hus in 1415, as he watched an old woman stagger up to add an extra bit of wood to the pyre on which he was being burned for heresy; and the same sort of brainless dedication may be seen on the faces of the pious pro-lifers marching and chanting at church-sponsored demonstrations.

Many of these same marchers, it has often been noted, show a curious lack of interest in extra-uterine life and the needs of already-born babies, children, and adolescents. By the same token, they often devoutly cherish the death penalty, which, whatever its Christian theological status, has a lot of solid support from the otherwise obsolete Old Testament.

Regardless of the specific sexual question, the immensely numerous, powerful, and vocal American Christian right will *always* be wrong. Pick a position, any position: Sex education should be given only in the home (public schools, riddled as they are by liberal relativism, can't impart values); no condoms should ever be distributed anywhere (Catholics like that one too); homosexuality isn't genetic, but freely chosen (though no one knows why); giving the HPV vaccine to prepubertal girls will only fan the flames of their latent promiscuity; gay men must never be Boy Scout leaders; no US government aid to women's health programs can ever mention the word "abortion"; Christians can't be feminists, and vice versa; stem cell research slaughters hecatombs of tiny humans, etc.

Both the main body of the Christian sexual crusaders (groups like American Family Association, National Right to Life, the Family Research Council, Focus on the Family, etc.) and the lunatic-fringers (the Quiverfull movement, Operation Rescue) are fueled by a murky mix of patriarchal nostalgia (whence the call for Christian wives to "surrender"), standard-issue Puritan misogyny (quick, name one nationally known woman minister), fear of the "Secular City," heady political power, and no doubt—on the part of some members—pangs of guilt over earlier moral lapses.

The net result of this retarded campaign and other forms of American irrationality is that the USA (and especially the red states) leads the First World in such dubious categories as teen pregnancies, STDs, illegitimacy, *and* those classical conservative taboos, abortion and divorce. But let the preachers (and their lay deputies) orate. One of these days (or decades, in a century or so) their rationally challenged flocks might just begin to suspect that wild extrapolations from misunderstood "proof texts" don't prove anything, and the reverend doctors of divinity dispensing sexual wisdom are actually quacks. As always, what a stupid country.

Chapter 24

Had Enough?

> In vain, in vain—the all-composing hour
> Resistless falls: The Muse obeys the Pow'r.
> She comes! she comes! the sable throne behold
> Of Night primeval, and of Chaos old!
> Before her, Fancy's gilded clouds decay,
> And all its varying rainbows die away.
> Wit shoots in vain its momentary fires,
> The meteor drops, and in a flash expires.
> As one by one, at dread Medea's strain,
> The sick'ning stars fade off th' ethereal plain;
> As Argus' eyes by Hermes' wand oppress'd,
> Clos'd one by one to everlasting rest;
> Thus at her felt approach, and secret might,
> Art after Art goes out, and all is Night.
>
> —Alexander Pope, *The Dunciad*, IV, 627-640

No jeremiad could do justice to the Niagara of absurdities—some merely stupid, some richly amusing, some downright criminal, some an amalgam of all three—flooding over American life and culture, not least of all because new ones are always springing up. This book has tried to tally and whack a cross-section of American nonsense, idiocy, vice, whatever; but in the immortal words of Rabbi Tarfon (inscribed in shortened form around the central building on my campus), "The day is short, the task is great, . . . the workers are lazy," and, alas, the Master so hopefully envisaged by Rabbi T. as goading those workers on hasn't been seen or heard from in ages. So, *faute de mieux*, here's a brief alphabetical catalog of topics that have, to be sure, been noticed and decried before, but are still worthy of further execration. As for the individuals on this *odi et arceo* list, they've been chosen not simply, or even primarily, for the various forms of obnoxiousness or fatuity that they embody, but for the large or small armies of fans, supporters, groupies, etc. that they've garnered in our free-market society. Absurdity is much harder to take once it gets popular. In case after case, not only *can* tens of millions of Americans be wrong, they *are* so beyond the slightest shadow of a doubt.

* * * * *

You Call This a Culture?

- adult offender status for children and juveniles (how else can you get revenge?)
- Afrocentrism—Molefi Kete Asante, Leonard Jeffries, et al. (fantasy social science)
- American "health care"—"Payment is expected before treatment"
- *American Idol* (but where is our King Josiah?)
- ambulance chaser ads ("Hurt in an accident recently"?)
- amusement parks (Inferno with rides)
- Ann Coulter (born, like Aphrodite, from the severed genitals of Joe McCarthy)
- "associates" (as in big-box-stores) (America's serfs—their gloomy faces say it all)
- Bada-Bing-style boob jobs and their fans (love those cantaloupe breasts)
- Bawa Walters (queen of the overachieving non-entities—see Larry King)
- beauty contests (T. & A. PLUS piano-playing and opinions on ecology!)
- bestsellers (junk food for the frontal lobe)
- Big Pharma (the ultimate non-discount Pusher)
- Bill Kristol, (Alfred E. Neumann without the wisdom)
- Bill O'Reilly (Keith Olbermann's runaway Worst Person in the World)
- bling (yobs need jewelry too)

Had Enough? 113

- Book of Mormon (and its besotted readers from Mitt Romney to Warren Jeffs)
- "bra-burner" (the stupid word itself, not the practically nonexistent person)
- Cable Shopping Network (consumerist liturgies for shut-ins)
- candy/cereal/cookie aisles in supermarkets (feeding our pyorrheal sweet tooth)
- canned hunting , exotic game farms (and most hunters, come to think of it)
- Catholic S. C. justices Scalia, Thomas, Roberts, Alito (wrong on everything)
- CEO compensation packages (gotta keep our oinkers singing contentedly)
- Charles Krauthammer ("Physician, heal thyself"—fat chance)
- Christian Science (Mary Baker Eddy's world-class oxymoron)
- Christmas Specials (God damn them, every one)
- Civil War re-enactments and Civil War buffs (tragedy as farce—again)
- college fraternities (cosy lodges for super-sized australopithecines)
- Concerned Women for America (concerned justice might break out somewhere)
- country music singers (with cowboy hats, bogus twangs, etc.)
- creationists (living proof that evolution doesn't necessarily mean progress)
- cryonics (Ted Williams' head, and such)
- death penalty enthusiasts (especially the Christian variety), ¡Viva la muerte!
- DHS color-coded Threat Levels (national security for kindergartners)
- Dennis Miller (failed sports announcer, fascist buffoon)
- Donald Trump (the whole insufferable franchise)
- epidemic obesity (the worse the food, the more of it they eat)
- "faith-based" programs (Jesus redeems, churches clean up)
- First Ladies (women still treasured as decorative accessories)
- Focus on the Family (Dobson's Choice for conquering militant feminism)
- food courts, feeding the multitudes by the rivers of Babylon
- Fox News (*Pravda* for Neolithics)

- funeral parlors (also embalming, wakes, etc.—holding on to corpses for dear life)
- gay "conversion" programs (magical gene-override, for the Pentateuch's sake)
- Girls Gone Wild (vomit-flavored college orgies)
- "grief counsellors" (a job all humans are supposed to perform)
- Halloween (the second-most lucrative "festival" in the year)
- "heroes" (somehow they're everywhere now)
- horror films (the audiences are the scariest part)
- Hummers (bring a little bit of the Iraq War to YOUR neighborhood)
- J.C. Watts, Ron Christie (black GOP-ers, steppin' and fetchin' for The Man)
- Jerry Lewis (the unamusing, but fabulously corrupt California Republican)
- Jews for Jesus (Messianic Christians, the last word in bad taste)
- Joe Scarborough (*this* is what we send to Congress?)
- Joel Osteen (Boy Wonder and smiley-faced, purveyor of Christianity Lite)
- Judge Judy (Honorable Mention to Joe Brown, Greg Matthis), pseudo-solon
- Karen Hughes (clueless ambassadress, *la Tejanita* talks to lady Muslims)
- Karl Rove (porcine Republican Rain Man)
- Laura Ingraham (Catholic convert and scourge of the gay lifestyle)
- Larry King (king of the overachieving non-entities—see Bawa Walters)
- Las Vegas (except as self-parody)
- Latino baseball players making the sign of the cross in the batter's box
- lawn-worshipers (pray for weeds)
- Lawrence Kudlow and Company (the Gadarene swine at play)
- libertarians (real estate agents for conservative Cloudcuckooland)
- Liberty U., Oral Roberts U., Bob Jones U. (a different kind of "fools for Christ")

Had Enough? 115

- "lifestyle" (and anybody phony or fatuous enough to have one)
- megachurches (Lakewood, Willow Creek, etc.), Christian bread and circuses
- Mexican border Minute Men (Full-blooded Yahoos on patrol)
- Miller beer (and other tasteless liquids meant for shipping, not sipping)
- Mount Rushmore (*res ipsa loquitur*: monumental, shameful folly)
- music videos (operettas for illiterates)
- neocons (one good reason for Jewish guilt)
- NASCAR (and its cretinous hordes, cheering the most popular sport in the USA)
- NCAA "student athletes" (muscular part-time tourists of the classroom)
- Oklahoma (and most things in it, starting with James Inhofe and Tom Coburn)
- "paintings" by Thomas Kinkade, schlockmeister of the moment
- penis enlargement ads (laughable, but imagine the nightmare if they worked)
- Phyllis Schlafly (evil octogenarian and lifelong enemy of the ERA)
- pit bulls (and the cult of the ferocious hound—man, those streets are *dangerous*!)
- Operation Rescue (there just aren't enough miserable teen moms and kids?)
- *Playboy* bunnies (Hugh Hefner's clones of Abishag the Shunnamite)
- Pledge of Allegiance (Under *whom*? With liberty and justice for *whom*?)
- power boats (got big bucks and tons of gas to waste?)
- Professor John Woo (torture-enabler, Constitution-dismantler)
- Promise Keepers (pep rallies for the patriarchy)
- Rachel Ray (the cult and the jabbering nullity at its core)
- Reality TV (*canis a non canendo*)
- rodeos (the Wild West returns, unfortunately)
- Rose Bowl Parade (technical brilliance, utter California vacuity)

- Route 17, New Jersey (el Camino Real of consumerism)
- Saturday morning cartoons (kids begin a lifetime of stupefaction)
- Scientology (and anyone who can say the word without giggling or snorting)
- Sean Hannity (professional Irish-Catholic ignoramus)
- shock jocks (middle-aged men acting like Beavis and Butt-Head)
- slaughterhouses (The Temple of Doom for millions of helpless animals—and not a few workers)
- St. Patrick's Day (American-style: greenish auto-eroticism for pseudo-Celts)
- Senator John McCain ("Bomb bomb Iran, Bomb bomb Iran" vocalist)
- Sex Respect (and other Christian abstinence programs—just pretend to say no)
- soap operas (heavy-breathing adventures for people who need to get a life)
- Southern Baptist Convention (substitutionary atonement and all that)
- Super Bowl (death by a million hypes)
- SUVs (chariots for chuckleheads)
- tarty tweenie fashions (bridging the gap between JonBenet and Paris Hilton)
- tattoos and body-piercings (tribal markings for deracinated savages)
- teen boot camps (Jesus-flavored gulags)
- Texas Rattlesnake Round-up (cf. *The Simpsons'* Springfield Snake Whacking Day)
- "the culture of life" (as opposed to liberal death-worship)
- theme parks (The Holy Land Experience, Orlando, FL, for example)
- The New York Post (Rupert Murdoch's used toilet paper)
- *The Passion of the Christ* (theandric red meat for Evangelicals)
- The Pentagon budget (it gives the word "sin" new meaning)
- *The Price Is Right* (and all game shows, where berserk adults squeal for toys)
- Tom Tancredo (even *The National Review* called him an idiot.)
- Tucker Carlson (political gossip pretending to be cub reporter)

- University of Phoenix (MBA's cut down the groves of Academe to make sawdust)
- USA Patriot Act (the Texas Taliban triumphs)
- Veterans Day (it should still be Armistice Day)
- video games (brain-zapping feedback loop)
- *Wall Street Journal* editorial-page (the plutocracy's bitch earning her keep)
- Wal-Mart (including the Walton family bunker in Bentonville, Arkansas)
- weather reports (too long, too boring. but blessedly non-controversial)
- white bread, frozen pizza, etc. (manna in the American culinary wilderness)
- White Republicans (3 basic categories: 1) fools , 2) knaves, 3) both)
- World Wrestling Federation (proud sponsor of psychomachias)
- zero-tolerance policies (and the morons who boast about them)

Well, this game could go on forever. Every reader will have his or her own poisonous list, which will constantly change, like the rosters of NFL teams, as current modes of ludicrousness—and worse, much worse—give way to newer ones (songs like "Feelings" supplanted by tunes like "Memory" from *Cats*), and some new Lawrence Welk Show or Operation Iraqi Freedom slouches toward Bethlehem to be born. The crucial question is: how do such lists differ from mere proliferating catalogs of Pet Peeves, the cluster of merely tedious, or at least non-lethal discontents bound to be produced by any civilization?

Let the reader decide, but I'd (obviously) rate American culture as at least seriously dysfunctional. Americans themselves are a cheerful, well-intentioned lot; but the culture they've created and that's created them is quite literally a bloody mess. Of course, crying, or bellowing, out "That does it!" does precious little, i.e., essentially nothing, to change the situation. But then that's the whole point of "desperate reflections": after thinking things over (and finding only a tiny minority who realize how bad things are), one might well become convinced that there's no (real) hope.

True, but there's always the Bronx cheer.

About the Author

Peter Heinegg was born in 1942 in Brooklyn to family that was one-quarter Jewish, one-half Austrian, and (thanks to a series of accidents) 100% Catholic. He attended Regis H.S. in Manhattan and entered the Jesuits in 1959, where he studied as a seminarian until 1966. He has an A.B. (English, 1965) from Fordham University and a Ph.D. (Comp. Lit., 1971) from Harvard. He has taught literature, mostly at Union College in Schenectady, N.Y., for thirty years, where he is a professor of English. He is married with two grown children. He has translated about 50 books (mostly on religion and theology) and written numerous essays, personal and otherwise, all of which may be obtained by inquiring at heineggp@union.edu. He has written *Better Than Both: The Case for Pessimism* (University Press of America, 2005); *Oh God! (And Other Follies): Essays on Religion* (UPA, 2006); and *Oh Wait—Now I Get It* (UPA, 2007).